Nectar of Nondual Truth

CONTENTS

10 Vivekananda & His Western Women Followers
by Linda Prugh
As everyone familiar with the philosophies of Sankhya and other Vedic religions will say, the number five holds an important place among them. Relative to this fact, five very unique souls were directly involved with Swami Vivekananda and his salutary work, and they were all women – strong and bold women who were pioneers of Vedanta in its earliest stages of dissemination in the West well over a century ago.

13 Nivedita: The Dedicated One
by S. Jagadishan
Back in 2007, this article appeared in *Nectar of Nondual Truth* as an offering from the late Mr. S. Jagadishan, and we are very happy to see it reach print again, a decade hence....

15 The Invisible Thread
by Sindhu & Joyesh Bagchi
Of all the interested souls in the West who made their way to the great Light of Swami Vivekananda after his arrival here in 1893, Sister Nivedita holds perhaps the uppermost tier of status in terms of both dedication and service rendered. She did not just go to India to offer assistance like some more popular women of recent times, she took India as her own country and gave her entire being to its upliftment – so much so that the Indian people of today revere her and count her among them.

25 Undying Fealty to Jnanam
by Babaji Bob Kindler
The seers of India, and indeed all religious traditions, hold a special place in their hearts and minds for Self-Knowledge, knowing as they do that, as Sri Krishna states in the Bhagavad Gita, it has no peer as a purifier for souls.

32 I Have a Mother
by Suzanne Schier-Happell
Mention of the dedicated Western women of early Vedanta cannot help but call to mind Sri Sarada Devi, modern India's Divine Incarnation of the Mother of the Universe. These fortunate women who met Her found their true Mother – Kali in human form.

37 The Law of Consequences
by Pravrajika Vivekaprana
Along profound philosophical lines, the topic of Karma receives a deep inspection by a beloved Pravrajika of the Sarada Math. All that remains now is for seekers to become keenly aware of the workings of karma and make changes that will better their lives.

40 Code of Conduct for Jain Householders
by Swami Brahmeshananda
Adding to his series of well-researched articles on the Jain tradition, a revered swami elucidates on the requirements of dedicated Jain householders, which are as austere as the rules laid down for monks.

44 American Ideals Through the Lens of Vedanta
by Annapurna Sarada
In a world whose streams of humanity are rushing towards hoarding materials and resources for purposes of pleasure and comfort, care must be taken to ensure the possession of core values. For what are possessions and comforts if one is devoid of purity and character?

48 Vedanta 101: pg 20, Vivarta & Viveka pg 48, The Sanctity of Childbirth
by SRV Associations
SRV Association's attracting and popular heading, "Hearing Vedanta," returns again as "Vedanta 101," offering two articles on subjects that beg explanation and implementation into the lives of sincere seekers.

"In this darksome time of the soul's misdirection, where gross physical preoccupations threaten even sacred spiritual atmospheres, it is refreshing to return to the primordial Source and encounter authentic Yoga as the ancient seers of India knew and practiced it."

Publisher's Page

Sarada Ramakrishna Vivekananda – SRV Associations
"Setting the feet of humanity on the path of Universal Truth."

Notes on an Advaitic Journal

At the basis of Advaita as the philosophy of Shankara and his gurus, there is Advaita as experience. Advaita as experience represents that supreme place where all diversity merges in its Essence. It is not combatant or immiscible with qualified or dualistic approaches, but rather provides them their place of consummate arrival. Where actual practice rather than mere book learning is emphasized, where religion, philosophy and spirituality are not separate from one another, where knowledge and love, reason and devotion, are never divorced from each other, there does the truth of authentic nonduality effloresce.

Historically speaking, experiential Advaita originated with the ancient Rishis. Therefore, the Upanisads contain the nondual truths of the Vedas which declare: idam mahabhutam anantam aparam vijnanaghana eva, *"This great Being is endless and without limit. It is a mass of indivisible Consciousness only."*

SRV Associations & Universality

The SRV Associations are part of a worldwide movement of spiritual aspirants devoted to the study and practice of Vedanta and Divine Mother Wisdom. The ideals of this ancient pathway to God, exemplified in the lives of Sri Sarada Devi, Sri Ramakrishna and Swami Vivekananda, are the original and eternal perfection of the Soul and its inherent oneness with Reality, the manifesting of divinity in our lives, selfless service of all beings as God, and reverence for the ultimate unity of all sacred traditions. To this end our purpose is to study, worship, and contemplate Truth so that spirituality may flourish. This is the Advaitic way — *"None else but Self, none other than Mother."*

Nectar's Mission — *Advaita-Satya-Amritam*

In Sanskrit, *amrita*, nectar also means Immortality – and this is, indeed, what we are offering: opportunities to become aware of this Amrita that is our very Essence via the rarefied teachings from Vedanta and the World Religions and Philosophies that appear in each issue of Nectar.

Nectar of Non-Dual Truth is SRV Associations' heartfelt offering of highest Wisdom to the human community. It is the sincerest form of love and service we know to disseminate non-dual Truth and teachings which transmit pure knowledge, pure love, and true universality. Through Nectar we are working out SRV's mission of spiritual upliftment and education. Please join us; this is a universal movement.

Keeping Nectar in Print

Nectar is a free magazine that can be ordered in printed form online at www.srv.org, and it can also be viewed online. (play.google.com/books) However, substantial donations are needed every year to maintain this publication in print. Why is this important?

1 – Printed Nectars are best for person to person and organization to organization dissemination of these ennobling teachings that deepen one's own spiritual life and engender knowledge of, acceptance, and reverence for all other paths.

2 – Only printed copies can reach those who do not have access to online viewing, including prison inmates, who are a particular focus of SRV's social seva.

Use the subscription/donation form provided at the back of this issue to send a check or credit card payment to SRV Associations, P.O. Box 1364, Honokaa, HI., 96727, or donate online at www.srv.org. Your donations are tax deductible.

With reverent gratitude, we heartily thank the contributing writers of this issue of Nectar of Nondual Truth, who have so graciously and selflessly shared the wisdom of their respective traditions and practices.

Staff of Nectar of Nondual Truth

Publisher
Sarada Ramakrishna Vivekananda Associations
an Annual Publication
For more information concerning the SRV Associations or Nectar of Nondual Truth please contact:
SRV Associations, PO Box 1364, Honoka'a, HI 96727
Phone: (808) 990-3354
e-mail: srvinfo@srv.org   website: www.srv.org
Nectar Subscription is on a donation basis only

No part of this publication may be reproduced or transmitted in any form without permission from the publisher. Entire contents copyright 2017. All Rights Reserved. ISSN 1531-1414

Editor
Babaji Bob Kindler

Associate Editor
Annapurna Sarada

Production
Lokelani Kindler

Cover Image:
Design: Prakasha Ben Cavalcanti
Photo, Bridge of the Gods:
Babaji Bob Kindler

Acknowledgement
Image of Ramakrishna's Disciples
Courtesy of Vedanta Press
800-816-2242

Contributing Writers
Pravrajika Vivekaprana
Swami Brahmeshananda
S. Jagadishan
Sindhu & Joyesh Bagchi
Suzanne Schier-Happell
Linda Prugh
Annapurna Sarada

EDITORIAL

A keenly vibrant and grateful world of conscious living beings who revere religion, philosophy, and spirituality, and who count themselves as lovers of Divine Reality on earth, has recently completed celebrating the 150th anniversary of the birth of that incomparable soul, Swami Vivekananda. And by the looks of it, it will take much more than another 150 years for the world to awaken to just who it was who came amongst them in that august form. Was it Buddha? Was it Lord Siva? Was it Jesus come again? Or was it an integrated combination of these great souls, including others, who graced this material loka – an atmic amalgam of earth-shaking proportions and ramifications?

To answer more fully these intriguing questions, inquiry into the lives of a few of the Western women who met him in his recent incarnation as the Divine Lord coming into human form, attended by powerful incarnations of Shakti bent upon lifting up the very physical level of existence itself into transcendent spiritual dimensions, can be made.

And that is also what *Nectar of Nondual Truth* aspires to in this issue, replete with articles by some of today's followers of this exceptional personage, many of them women. The early herald of this Western contingent of fearless and faithful female followers was Sister Nivedita, whose own 150 year Sesquicentennial is upon us this year. By her given family title, Margaret Noble, she was well-named even in English, being of noble bearing and qualities, both.

Under the guidance of Swami Vivekananda for seven years of her life, to whom she surrendered completely via the traditional form of the unique guru/shishya relationship so precious to Mother India, she was also of noble attainments. Her notable story is now one of historic record and indelible memory which singles her out as an exceptional Karma-yogini who, along with serving India's children, gracefully handled the difficult racial, caste-ridden, cultural barriers that impeded India when she was present there. And even today it warmly ingratiates her to Western people who need a perfect exemplar of such deep and "noble" self-surrender. Her sacrifice shows what is mandatory in order to enter and complete all the requisites for attaining an enlightened state of mind and an active spiritual life. At the same time it reveals to the typical purse-proud, money-maddened Westerner, "drunk with new wine," the need to rid oneself of the arrogance that fuels the unripe human ego and stymies its progress towards gaining real qualities such as spiritual wisdom, nonviolence, compassion for the sufferings of others, and selfless service of God in mankind.

The collection of articles gathered lovingly in this issue of *Nectar* extend their sweep into the radiant regions of the Four Yogas, brought current in this day and age by Swami Vivekananda. In this darksome time of the soul's misdirection, where gross physical preoccupations threaten even sacred spiritual atmospheres, it is refreshing to return to the primordial Source and encounter authentic Yoga as the ancient seers of India knew and practiced it. Modern seers like Swamiji saw the need and took the trouble to bring it West and spread it broadcast here so that pretensions around true spiritual life and practice could be effectively annulled, and pretenders — like those spurious yogis who wrote books filled with occult powers that today mislead seekers after Truth — be recognized and rejected. For, body-based hathayoga, food faddism, affectatious dancing to impress and attract others, repetitious chanting of a few Sanskrit names devoid of any comprehension of their real import, and overtaxing the body, brain, and nervous system with marathon-minded meditation retreats when the human mind is still full of impurities and desires for the world – all of this is unwise, is merely personality posturing in the name of true spirituality. Instead, let's study this modern Luminary, Swami Vivekananda, and get much better clues as to how to proceed with sadhana.

There is a better path for present-day Western people, and it proceeds via the Four Yogas, deeply studied and carefully guided. To this radiant road SRV Associations and *Nectar of Nondual Truth* pledges its own dedication, as it has been doing for twenty-five years. A great part of its inspiration, and the outright saving grace of this age, is that the Order which Swami Vivekananda founded in the name of his Guru, Sri Ramakrishna, has focused selflessly on interpreting and presenting to the people of this day and time countless revealed scriptures from India's eternal storehouse of Sanatana Dharma – even translating them lucidly into many languages. Many biographies of Great Souls have been written as well, by devotees and onlookers whose lives were transformed by them. This path now lies open to all, and some six million souls can attest to this.

Om Peace, Peace, Peace
Babaji Bob Kindler

NECTAR OF ADVAITIC INSTRUCTION

Questions from Our Readers

What is Enlightenment? According to Vedanta, it is the constant remembrance of the fact that all is Brahman, including time, space, living beings, and the world. When this key remembrance is threatened by ignorance caused by forgetfulness, the wise seeker takes refuge in the teachings of Dharma.

"You have mentioned in some of your teachings that, once initiation is taken, Liberation is already at hand. The only thing left is for the mind to be awakened. Will you please elaborate on this? What is the difference in the two?"

This is a good question, and a fine subject to elaborate on. Of course, the Soul, *Atman*, is "ever-free, never-bound," and so is always in a liberated condition. We must always bear that in mind. But that is from the standpoint of freedom itself, once realized. From the standpoint of this supposed bondage we are weighed down by, we are at present walking a path that leads *"….from lower truth to Higher Truth – Asato ma sad gamaya."* The awakening will be by stages. That is, as the mind sloughs off its impositions and neutralizes its karmas, the ever-free state dawns upon it in increments until it perceives its Eternal Perfection. Now, this process cannot move forward and culminate until we actually set our feet on the path and accomplish the requisite practices that are required of us. Once the path is accepted and the *mantra* given, the *karmas* of the mind start unwinding. This process itself will take longer or go faster according to the amount of *karma* present in the mind. The good side of this is, if the *mantra* is powerful and the path is lofty, then no amount of *karma* will be too much to exhaust in a single lifetime….even two. To say the least, any lifetimes taken after this one will be attended with more light, simply due to the presence of the *mantra* and the grace of the Guru.

"There are times when I cognize the Mother as a being such as Sri Durga or Her four-armed form and other times when She is more of a power or principle of fearlessness. When fearlessness and the will to overcome doubt, weakness, the gunas (esp. rajas and tamas), and just be in one state of awareness rises and is active in the mind, I think it is She (Her Shakti powers) that is doing so. So to what extent is the Divine Mother really a Truth principle of the relative plane, who while having infinite forms and dynamic power, is really beyond name and form?"

To the fullest extent. She is essentially formless, and even when She enters into form, that form is formless as well – like a Divine Energy, say, *Kundalini Shakti*. Contemplating Her with form, and many-armed, etc., is an early phase, and natural at the beginning. Most beings stop there. But to uncover Her deepest secrets is to go within towards the realms of causal nature, and eventually and ultimately to *Advaita*, nondual Truth.

"When saying that the world is unreal, is it meant that the world is literally unreal? That it is strictly an appearance, like the rope and the snake analogy? It amazes me to think of this being the case because the world seems to be convincingly real; however, when considering the rope and snake analogy, I can see how the world to the majority of human beings is taken to be the reality. Could you possibly comment on this some more?"

The word "unreal" is a bit misleading. Really, in the Vedantic context, it means ever-changing. As Christ said it, you cannot build your house on sand. The shifting sands of *maya*, then, will not support a real life. Thus, the world may as well be literally unreal. But not unreal as, say, a mirage in a desert is unreal. The world is more persistent than that, as it has the thinking (*sankalpic*) power of billions of souls behind it.

And it is because of this fact that great luminaries like Lord Buddha encouraged truth-seeking followers to go beyond their ancestors, for heaven, earth, and hell are all full of beings who are caught in the configuration of *Samsara* — which consists of thinking the world to be real, even the only Reality. So give it up, say the great ones.

"Is Divine Mother transcendent of form and formlessness?"

Yes, this too is true. She nevertheless works through both in order to lead souls to the ultimate state of Awareness. Limited thinkers have opined that this *maya* is Hers, and that She bewitches souls with it. It may be true in part, but for those who do not want to be enchanted anymore She reveals the supreme condition of Pure Consciousness. That is why the Great Souls have *Samadhi, Nirvana, Satori, Kaivalya, Asamprajnata*, while others do not.

"Is the Mother's Lila only limited to Her devotees? Her Lila is transcendent of dualities, correct? Can you explain how the Lila of the Mother is different from the way fundamentalist Christianity views the involvement of God in the world? It would seem to me that the Lila of the Mother is always leading one towards the Atman knowingly or unknowingly. Whether She creates, preserves, or destroys beings, nations, families, relationships, is it ultimately for the Highest Nondual Good?"

Lila is Her way of expressing divinity in the realm of form, and therefore is not transcendent of dualities. However, the dualities that appear there are serving the Lord and Mother, and

not binding Their votaries. As Sri Ramakrishna has stated about the world: *"Here I can eat, drink, and be merry."* It was all sport to Him, whereas to others – even those who may pretend *lila* – they will fall again and again into suffering and delusion, with pleasure seeking as the point of life mixed in, periodically.

As for Christianity, the seeking for heaven could be called a type of *lila*, and *"....sporting in the fields of the Lord"* is also mentioned in scripture. However, India's way of interpreting Jesus's teachings and method focus on His renunciation of the world rather than its enjoyment, as He, Himself, emphasized. His lila, like so many other luminaries, had suffering to bear. Transcendence, then, as India teaches, is part of the play.

"Is the lila of the Mother present even in deluded beings addicted to the world and sense-life? If so, is it only a matter of the separate 'I' that causes this delusion? Once beings come to surrender their ego, will they come to realize it was always Mother's lila?"

Yes, and no. Authentic *lila* is a rare experience, only vouchsafed to those who have done what is necessary to raise their consciousness to that level where everything is *Brahman*. Still, the divine play is going on all around, at all times. The worldly are simply unable to see it or participate in it. If, through Her Grace, they suddenly have an experience of it, then they feel truly aware. But it passes quickly, and gets forgotten amidst the weights and distractions of *maya*.

"I have been working on steadying my devotion. Yesterday the practice went quite well. I was thinking about how much work there is here in the university. What is there to gain from all this work if there is no such thing as helping the world? Surely, it is a blessing to ourselves. We do Mother's work, but ignorantly call it our own. This has become quite evident to me in the past couple of days. Is this what Mother wants me to do, to worship her through secular studies? Are there some forms of worship that Mother prefers better than another? It seems like I should find this out from Her."

As to your question whether Mother wants you to worship Her through secular studies, that is a "toss-up," as they say. As we can see in the case of intellectuals of the day, they are quite worldly and have no sense of the Divine in them, and in others, yet. That is why so many of them are supporting Western science and are "in bed" with politics rather than protesting wars, bombing, and other suffering causing and karma-forming actions. Divine Mother would certainly not want anyone to worship Her in this way. The wars She wants us to wage are within our own minds, and if we gain victory there She will be most pleased with us and grant us higher Wisdom – not just secular knowledge.

Now, on the other hand, your studies are a chance to discipline your mind and gain control over it. Since life is full of variances, and until we gain that especial boon of peace and bliss in life that is so hard to attain, we must face off with these difficulties and hardships. But for the devotees of the Lord and Mother, this face-off is not just to forbear suffering (which is a good lesson too), but to attain mastery over the world and all phenomena. For instance, if I had not learned English in high school – as much as I disliked high school – I would not be writing books now on spirituality that can and may benefit other beings.

So, and obviously, others – the worldly – only experience their God-given awareness and its intelligence dully and unconsciously, with no ultimate Goal or meaningful purpose; it is all just to gain money and objects for pleasure. Thus, the student of today must make sure to include spirituality in their schooling.

"In Yoga Vasishtha, Rama says: 'Recently I went on a pilgrimage. During this period a trend of thought has taken hold of me, robbing me of all hope in this world. My heart begins to question: what do people call happiness and can it be had in the ever-changing objects of this world? All beings in this world take birth but to die, and they die to be born again! I do not perceive any meaning in all these transient phenomena which are the roots of suffering and sin.' Now, to me, Rama's thoughts make sense, and I tend to agree with what he says, but some other person might ask: 'Why does there have to be any meaning to the world and its transient phenomena? Maybe there need be no meaning in the way things are.' If someone asks this question to me, I don't know what to respond. What is your answer to such a question/comment?"

It is not only the careless person who concludes that there is no meaning to life; it is also the spiritual person who knows this. Remember what I wrote in my last message, about *sattva* and *tamas* looking the same? But there is a vast difference under the surface. Under the surface of things, Sri Ram knows that there is specific meaning in everything, in every event, every appearance, every person, i.e., in all of existence. The careless person does not know or see this, and thereby lives a frivolous life – a meaningless life, yes?

We could talk about karma some more here. There may not be any deep meaning in life and its repetitive rounds, but there is *karma* to bear in it, is there not? That fact alone lends sudden meaning to the spiritual aspirant's life because he/she does not want to come back here and experience more of these fruitless rounds of mundane existence. He/she does not want to suffer anymore, nor enjoy either if suffering is the result. Peace leading to bliss is the path of the sensitive soul here on Earth. Nothing can compete with it here, and nothing compares to it in any other of the three worlds either.

Ironically, then, you will find meaning in Life when you find that life is meaningless. That is why Jesus told his apostles that if they loved their life they would lose it, but if they hated their lives they would get Eternal Life instead. Worldly life is empty, but *dharmic* life is full. People do not know this, or find this out, only because of their attachment to mundane life. That is called *maya, samsara*, relativity, worldly life, sensual life, and so forth. But moral life, *dharmic* life, divine life, and finally Eternal Life — those are the real concerns and carriers of meaning for the sincere soul caught in the embodied condition.

"Sorry to have been out of touch for a week, but I have been sick. I am now better and back into my studies. There is so much to learn! Can you help me a little in this respect by explaining more about the mind at its three levels, and the 24 tattvas and its sets of fives? I am also interested in the niyama

called 'clinging to life.' So much of what you teach I find like pieces in a puzzle that I am putting together in this lifetime. I have played games before, but not one like this that is so engaging, and important."

I see you have written again. Sorry to hear about your illness. They come and they go in this embodied condition. What to say? The body gets sick; the *Atman* remains the same.

For the essential connections of Mind on its three levels — cosmic, collective, and individual — you would be well served to get my new book title, *Cosmic Quintuplications*. In the meantime, you can see and study the same in my earlier book called *Dissolution of the Mindstream*. Basically, Mind connects to its various levels via sets of fives, called *tattvas* in Sanskrit. The projection process of Mind goes on via this same process, called *sankalpa*. Details are to be gathered, then contemplated. Once accomplished, this ladder of expression can be used by the adept to get in and out of the body consciously at the time of birth and death, and also move to dreaming and deep sleep states consciously while still occupying the body. It is all fascinating, and a very ancient system in India.

Staying free of the desire for the fruits of action is one of the precepts of *Karma Yoga*, and is to be observed along with several other points of that path. In *Raja Yoga*, Patanjali gives out the teaching of *aparigraha* as one of the *yamas* of *Yoga*, to ensure that beginning aspirants do their best to reduce the exchange of goods and gifts with others that, when indulged in without proper discrimination, tend to cause the soul to forget its divine origin – what to speak of its past lifetimes. The idea is that if the parents can guide the soul in this way early on, when it is fresh from the disembodied state [see article on page 46, this issue], it can more easily remember its passage from past lifetimes. For those who do not get this early training – which describes most souls nowadays – they have to strike away conditionings (such as the habit of materialism and sensuality) later using spiritual practices. This is a "second best" scenario. Worst of all, as you know, is never finding the spiritual path at all, and that is due to engaging in "commerce," as you say, or put another way, worldliness. In such cases (the multitudes), day to day life simply leaches the *prana* out of the quotient, leaving people listless and dependant on insentient objects and insipid pleasures. Conclusion? "Do not covet the goods of anyone," as the *Ishavasyopanisad* states in its second sloka, and stay free of possession of and identification with matter and materials.

You ask also about clinging to life (*abhinivesha*) and the rest. These that you list are the five *kleshas* of *Yoga*. Learn to call them that, for once you put a label on such lists you are half way to mastering them. The mental posture to wear with regard to them is called *klesha-vinashana-asana*, or, "I will dissolve the five impediments to *Yoga*." Thus, when you assume such a posture, and follow through with implementing it, you are putting ignorance, egotism, attachment, aversion, and clinging to life on stark notice that their time as unwanted occupants in your mind is swiftly coming to an end. Now, keep this mental posture up day to day until they disappear completely. You would not want your body to slump all the time, would you? Poor posture? Well, the same is true of the mind; it must not be allowed to slump. Render it *"straight as a well-fletched arrow,"* as the Buddha says.

All this I send to you as guidance from afar. Better still will be when we are together again in the *dharmic* atmosphere, where so many of our problems and shortcomings simply disappear due to collective sadhana and Mother's Grace.

"Is the main reason for meditating on the 24 cosmic principles to realize that they were all projected out of the mind and thus be able to transcend them?"

In my way of teaching, yes, that is basically it. But there are earlier stages that lead to such transcendence, like meditating on each of them in inward ascending order so as to come upon hidden glitches or idiosyncrasies in the mind. The way we see the universe is in accordance with the condition of our mind. That is why, at a very late stage, one can actually see God in the universe, due to correcting the wrong perceptions that were in the mind when all things got projected. It is an ironing out process that, unfortunately, most of us have to accomplish in reverse fashion. That is, we should have manufactured our mental complex with a pure mind rather than a restless or confused or imperfect mind....like the seers, etc. So, live and learn, taking better embodiments with finer and finer intelligence in the mind!"

"While on holiday I started studying Nikhilananda's translation of the Bhagavad Gita. I was only able to get through the story, introductions, first chapter and part of the second chapter as I felt the need to read and reread it. Reading the stanzas brought up many things to contemplate and also several questions. I'll ask my 'first chapter questions' in this email and save the next chapter for when I get all the way through it a few times. The first one is around the portrayal (or lack thereof) of women in the writing. My feeling is that it is obviously written in a time and culture where women had no personal power and generally held a very low status in society. My assumption, given Atman is genderless and formless, is that the teachings, written only to include men in the 'important stuff', applies equally to women?"

Of course, you are right, since *Atman* has no gender. And from the outside, a Westerner might think that women were of low status in those times, but that refers only to worldly beings. It is much the same today among the worldly, that women are looked down upon and used by men. On the other hand, for example, there was *Draupadi*, the wife of the *Pandava* brothers, who was a major player in the *Mahabharata*, from which the Gita is excerpted. There were also many women *rishis* of the times too, like *Maitreyi* and *Gargi* – equal to and even surpassing the men in wisdom. Further, war is man's horrid business. The *Gita* is set against the *Kurukshetra* war. Thus, it is all about the men fighting. The women are back at home using better sense.

Second, there is significant time in the first chapter dedicated to *dharma* – both as one's "duty" and as the "law of his being." How does a person know what their *dharma* is and then follow it? If we are to cut to the chase and listen to beings like Sri Ramakrishna, then it is really everyone's *dharma* to realize God in this lifetime. If this is accepted as the Goal of human existence and embodiment, then the question becomes by what means am I to facilitate access to this Goal and realize it? This is where other *Gita* chapters that follow are important, as Sri

Krishna embarks upon discourses that show how work is to be accomplished *dharmically*, free of karma. Then it is to be transcended in stages by first giving up all actions that are against the ordinances of the scriptures while keeping only scripturally ordained works. Finally, all fruits are abandoned and one lives in an illumined state. But it all begins by giving up works that are *karma*-bearing. One has to persevere in the *dharma* for a time as well, so that old *karmas* are destroyed forever.

"In Indian culture there are castes that give direction on what your 'destined' path must be, but in Western culture most of the familial history is lost. These teachings have several points regarding dharma; they talk of the confusion that can occur trying to decide right from wrong, such as a *Kshatriya* killing in the right circumstances is his duty, but a *Brahmin* killing for any reason is sin. I recognize that the four castes expect a differing level of spiritual evolution within the ranks which leads to the 'kill or no-kill' scenario, but how does an individual today know what the right path is when it is generally more subtle than just go to battle or not? How does *dharma*, *adharma* and the 'decay of families' apply today?"

The matter is more complex today due to the entire system having to be applied to the Western mind. That mind is violent, selfish, materialistic, fearful, lacking in depth, etc. But if minds that are caught in this modern day dilemma will strive to reverse these tendencies, and do it with the teachings of *dharma* and intense *sadhana*, some success and forward progress can be made.

Though it is hard to say, the subject of families is important only if the family is *dharmic*. Beings come and go in and out of this world by the hundreds of thousands every year. It has been that way for endless cycles. But what is not seen in this cosmic flux is twofold: first, there are some beings that realize a higher station of consciousness and do not return to this earth; and second, there are also good *dharmic* people being born in this world – even fully realized luminaries like Vivekananda and Ramana Maharshi. Thus we are to know that there is a purveyor of absolute Goodness here, namely the Divine Mother, and by focusing on and worshipping Her all *karmas* get annulled.

"I was ruminating on the five *kleshas* of Yoga today and found that *asmita*, the second *klesha*, is all about confusion as to what to do and what not to do; one's mind, thoughts, energy, and senses all get confused. Thus, it is the unripe ego that leads us into confusion. Should we not surrender it up to Divine Mother, then, and ripen it? Further, in Ch. 1, vs. 46 the explanation says, '*If one sees evil, one must resist it.*' It discusses 'righteous action,' yet what this brings up in me is that this carte blanche 'righteous action' leads down the path of ridiculous, egoic, religious wars (like the ones we see occurring now). This means that one must discern the best form of 'resistance.' The challenge I see most is that the text then says it is 'all good' to kill a 'felon' – no questions asked – judge, jury, and executioner. Felons kill other men, steal lands, or steal wives. How does a human, confused by maya, decide what the course of action should be?"

This point is made in the context of protecting oneself, family, and country, from evil-minded beings. Yes, it may have been easier to discern who was evil and who was righteous in earlier times, but that does not excuse us or free us from following the path of righteousness. Since the *Atman* cannot be killed, and that is the ultimate Truth, then knowing that makes the relative laws clearer, and so too our duty. I teach in prisons several times a year. There, I notice that not one evil being ever comes to Vedanta class. There are some beings with bad *karma*, no doubt, who attend, but the evil are just not interested. This clear line of demarcation makes it a simple matter to divide the Divine from the Demoniacal – which is the title of Chapter 16 in the *Gita* that you must read.

"In Ch. 1, vs. 10 of the Gita, it discusses Bhishma who is on the side of the king, (grandfather to both King Duryodhana & Arjuna) as unlimited, and Bhima (Arjuna's brother) as limited. It feels like the verse and the explanation contradict each other. The verse makes sense, but I feel like I'm not understanding it because it feels like the explanation is backwards."

This is maya, and how it works. It will confuse us if we do not move to gain higher understanding, i.e., transcendence. The *Kurukshetra* battlefield itself, and the beings on it, are a prime example of how *maya* works. The cookie there has crumbled in such a fashion as to place some good beings on the bad side, and some bad beings on the good side. This is life; such utter nonsense happens all the time; you must have noticed. As they say nowadays, "Bad things happen to good people."

But the point of it all is not which side is right or wrong, or how the story turns out, or even the mixed *karmas* of everyone taking part in this play. The point is to see its (*maya's*) dangers and to get out of it *"as quickly as a young mother with a newborn baby in a house on fire."*

"How did the sense of ego, this 'I-ness,' come into being?"

Through root ignorance, or primal nescience. The real question should be, "How did it overpower the Soul and then perpetuate itself for so many lifetimes?" There are souls who come into existence for one lifetime only, see what is here, conclude that it is unreal, and immediately merge back into *Brahman* – never to embody again (*videhamuktis*). Now that deserves some contemplation, yes?

"While engaging in the process of viveka and moving toward or into the egoless Pure Consciousness, why not accept ego and allow it to function as one moves along? Does ego need to be denied to know Atman? If it's accepted, won't it be transformed as one moves inward, toward realization? To discipline the ego so it's not an impediment to sadhana through aligning its functioning with principles like the yamas and niyamas of Patanjala Yoga is a very different matter than a discipline that has as its end the elimination of the ego. Why eliminate it? Why fight that particular battle? In Buddhist thought, this shore and the other shore are understood to be the same in the end. Why not accept this at the beginning and seek realization from within this prior understanding of wholeness?"

What you ask here, or declare, is perfectly alright. Thakur used to advise maturing the ego so that it would not get in the way of deeper spiritual experiences to come. Perhaps what you

need to hear pertains to the ego at the level of *Nirvikalpa*, or *Asamprajnata*. Both in *Yoga* and *Vedanta*, the sense of separation will, or must, disappear in order that total immersion, or the seedless state, can occur. That is why, in *Sankhya*, the ego is a station that gets transcended as higher *tattvas* get encountered. You might look at it from the perspective of last night's sleep. In order for you to get into dreamless sleep you had to abandon the ego mechanism, and that is why you had no sense of separation, nor any sense of form, when you did. So, as a practice you may ripen away, but at the level of the highest attainment you must abandon all the rats must leave the sinking ship!

"I see viveka-khyati as a stage in the process of discrimination wherein one specifically separates Consciousness from its reflection in buddhi. Is this understanding correct? After separating Consciousness from its reflection in buddhi, are there yet subtler stages in the process of discrimination before one reaches the supreme realization where Atman stands alone?"

Yes, *viveka-khyati* is discriminating wisdom used in the subtle process of the separation of the *buddhi* from the *Purusha*. This is a stage of practice that happens generally at the fourth level of *Samprajnata Samadhi*, and it is necessary for the final stage of seedless samadhi — where *Atman* stands alone.

"The first manifestation of jiva as it comes into expression from the causal state is a reflection in buddhi. Is the sense of I-ness itself this first expression, or is I-ness just a characteristic of this reflection of Atman? In the second instance, I imagine buddhi to be like the surface of a lake; the Sun of Atman is reflecting in the lake and I-ness is simply a characteristic of this reflection."

Yes, your thinking here is sound. What gets left out in the philosophical explanation is that all of it is *Atman's* doing, so to speak. The sense of I-ness at that level is not gross *ahamkara*, but *sasmita samadhi*. There is really such great bliss there in the inception of the ego, not mentioned much in philosophy.

But for this to be so the *buddhi* is going to have to be clear and powerful, is it not? For, *Atman* is present in all beings, and in all things, but the being or thing is not aware of It in so many cases. That is why Consciousness, Awareness, has to be first, and must be singular. A lifetime or two of the practice of this singularity will clear the *buddhi* and the ego will ripen, and the entire process will be seen as the incarnating luminary sees it — as God entering into form and sporting there.

"When I look within to watch conditioned identity arising in me, I see at work the dynamic which appropriates objects as props for I-ness. It appears to be the case that I-ness is being literally manufactured from the stuff of the world. I'm wondering if it's accurate to use the term 'ahamkara' to denote I-ness itself? Or does this term better refer to the dynamic by which I-ness is generated? Could the term 'asmita' be used to refer to I-ness itself? If I'm off the mark here will you please clarify both the metaphysical questions raised and the meanings of the two terms, 'ahamkara' and 'asmita;' are those terms synonyms, or could 'asmita' relate more to I-ness as the reflection of Atman arising in buddhi, while 'ahamkara' might relate more to the generation of conditioned ego within active samsaric machinations?"

Yes, if you want to make the distinction, it is quite sound. The more important of the two perspectives is the one of dynamism, where the Real Self is emanating rays of consciousness that congeal into the sense of I-ness. That is how God gets into form, as it were. As Thakur said, the same sunlight reflects in thousands of dew-drops every morning, and much like that, consciousness manifests Itself in all beings.

Our only real task, then, is to remain aware of Awareness, conscious of Consciousness – and if we can do it here, in this very body, we can do it anywhere and everywhere.

"What is the best way to combine pranayama with japa?"

I would suggest that they not be combined. But they can be contemplated, philosophically, and that helps the mind. But it is better to do pranayama as purification, then japa as its own practice. Formless meditation, when the soul is prepared for it, is to be attempted as its own, salient state of being.

"What does Shankara mean by 'right action' in sloka 11 in the Vivekachudamani?"

The same thing that Lord Buddha means by right livelihood in his Eightfold Path. All the seers will agree that the way of action is both a stumbling block and a path to higher existence. It is a stumbling block when the art of inaction is not understood and practiced along with it. It is a pathway to higher existence when one uses it to gather knowledge from daily life, like extracting essence from one's experiences. Most beings do not do this, but just move mechanically from one happening to the next, never searching for meaning or making conclusions about what occurs to them. It is like bees gathering honey from various flowers. Some of the bees have a hive and a queen. Others are bereft of both. These latter have no where to deposit their honey or, put in *Bhagavad Gita* terms, do not do sacrifice. As Sri Krishna states, *"This world is not for the non-sacrificer, so how will any other world be available to them?"*

"Is it important to dig one deep well in terms of knowing a single scripture well? I'm finding that at times I get restless because there is so much to study and know in spiritual life and then end up not getting a lot memorized because of it. How should I balance studying the raja yoga and scriptures such as Vivekachudamani and Bhagavad Gita?"

The digging the deep well analogy is usually used for following a single path. But it applies here as well, with a single scripture. Really, the aspirant should take up (and in) many scriptures. The problem, or art of it, is time – when to take them up. If you find that it is all too much, that there are discrepancies in the approach of each causing confusion in your mind, then go back to the study of one only. What I am writing here applies to scriptures, however, not to books such as the *Gospel of Sri Ramakrishna*. You should read that all the time, even piecemealing it, *I-Ching* style, after the first thorough read through. In other words, some works complement each other, while others demand full attention on them alone.

Finally, if you have a living *guru* available to clear up appar-

ent contradictions, you may be able to study several at once – at least within a single religion. Another facet of this is phases of time. If you are young, or new to the tradition, you will want to take holy company (*sadhu-satsangha*) often. Taking retreats, attending upon the wise, and asking questions (*Atma-vichara*) will smooth out the overflow, and the seeming disparities.

"I started Patanjali's aphorisms. Can you please explain even more the meaning of chitta and vrittis, and how vrittis arise?"

These *vrittis*, thought vibrations, or *chitta*, are what the practitioner must master in the fifth limb of Yoga. Think, for instance, of an erratic flow of electricity and how it damages the component (like an appliance or a computer) through which it is moving. Then think of how nervous energy flowing through nerves – both physical and psychic – will cause damage to the brain and to the mind if it is not evened out through practice. The result is what people call "stress" nowadays. Vrittis can be dull (*tamasic*) and drag the mind down, or they can be frenetic (*rajasic*) and excite and confuse the mind. However, they can also be balanced and peaceful (*sattvic*) so as to both allow the mind to gain peace, and prepare it for higher states of awareness, called meditation and *samadhi* (seventh and eighth limbs).

"Why is Maya unknowable?"

Mainly because it is unreal. And everything about it that seems real is always changing. Name, form, time, space, and causation are all *maya*. Just look at how people take to these five and forget all else! Change is also *maya*, and just see how change is the spice of life and, further, how no one wants peace or is interested in changelessness, i.e., in God/*Brahman*. And through and after all of this, no one has been able to know *maya*. It just disappears as one approaches it – like those mirages of mud-puddles on the road in the distance as one drives nearer to them. The closer you get, the farther away they retreat. Just come to know *Brahman*. Then you will be able to detect the presence of *maya* in form. Finally, *maya* goes away at the time of *mukti*, never to return. It has an end for those who seek its end.

"How do we know if our renunciation of cravings is sincere?"

When they do not rise up anymore, and even if they do, it is easy to get past them. At first one will have to exert will power, and that helps to convince one of one's own strength and potential mastery over objects of desire. But soon thereafter no effort will be necessary. There may come next a phase of just observing them as they rise, and later a quick look at them as if they are a mirage, or a joke. Whatever the case, or phase, the attainment of natural renunciation is priceless – as we saw in the authentic *Paramahamsa*, Sri Ramakrishna.

"What is Ishvara/Ishvari?"

Isha means "chosen." Great Souls are chosen to oversee all the worlds, inner and outer, and all the beings that inhabit them, temporarily. *Ishvara* is the male, *Ishvari* is the female version. There are no higher personages in existence than *Ishvara/Ishvari*. When beings pray to or meditate upon God, they are really doing so to Ishvara/i. The formless *Brahman* has no ears to hear, you see, and no form to contemplate. One can only merge in That.

"The following sloka from the Bhagavad Gita is mentioned in the elucidation of verse 1: 'The yogi who strives with assiduity, purified from sins and perfected through many births reaches the Supreme Goal.' In what sense is the word sins used here. In other words, what are these sins?"

A better word than "sin" in English is "transgression." The Christians have ruined the word sin and turned it into a black mark on the soul, one that has eternal ramifications. Vedantists use the word "ignorance," (*avidya*), and wisely replace the Hell and Damnation scenario with the Law of *Karma*. Among other things, this takes God out of the praise and blame arena. As Holy Mother stated, *"We should neither praise nor blame God for what happens to us in life."* So, if the soul makes mistakes and accrues *karma*, then all it has to do is to purify said *karma* and be free again. However, this is accomplished by intense spiritual disciplines (*sadhana*), not by holy water and confessions.

These errors that the soul binds itself with come from thoughts, words, and deeds. To stop this freight train of *karma*, the best way is to purify the thoughts. Then words and deeds will be pure, and no *karma* will accrue. Freedom awaits that rare soul who controls the mind, then lets the body and senses follow.

"In a conversation with another devotee we were talking about learning the 24 cosmic principles. Neither of us were absolutely certain of the subject, but upon reflecting about it as you teach it in class, here are the reasons we came up with for learning this system: 1) it provides a system for practicing neti neti; 2) it gives a road map for how consciousness projected the universe and got embodied, and thus can be utilized to get into formless meditation; 3) by contemplating on the principles and system, one can detect fears and granthis and destroy such impositions. Thus, it can be used to thin the curtain of nescience. It can also make connections on a subtle level that go beyond the ability of language to communicate."

Very good! You have listed the main points just fine.

"In the Divine Mother scriptures it is explained that Mother's lila manifests through the subtle and mysterious hidden centers of spiritual power called 'lotuses.' I have read about this, but I don't quite understand what these lotuses are and how they work. Can you please offer an explanation about these subtle centers and how Mother manifests through them?"

These *chakras*, as they are called, are spiritual vortexes of subtle energy, coursing within and leading to higher and deeper planes of Existence. Within these profound levels of pure Consciousness there is so much of Light, so much of Bliss, and so much of Truth. Embodied beings rarely feel any of this because they vibrate or dwell only at the three lower centers, or lotuses. These are, according to Sri Ramakrishna, equated to eating, drinking, and sex life. If that is all the human being is interested in, then he/she will not strive to awaken to these higher levels of Existence. If you can attend upon one of our Kundalini Yoga retreats, you will take in a lot about the *chakra* system.

Questions, observations and insights regarding problems in spiritual life or the issues of the day may be directed to Nectar's editorial staff at srvinfo@srv.org and will be duly addressed in succeeding issues.

◆ LINDA PRUGH

SWAMI VIVEKANANDA & HIS WESTERN WOMEN FOLLOWERS

Sister Nivedita, Swami Vivekananda's Irish disciple who gave her life completely to the upliftment of India's people, was pre-eminently qualified for the large brushstrokes of social change that she carried out through the sacred force of both a deep understanding and dedication to her spiritual master. It is no wonder that she is so well-remembered. However, she had four sister-disciples born of the West with whom she shared her toil, her inspiration, and challenges. They formed their own special community bound by their common love, faith, and service of Vivekananda and his mission in the West and in India. They spent time in each others' company and wrote diligently and frequently to each other, keeping themselves current on both the swami's activities and plans, and each other's progress in helping to actuate his mission in its countless ways. Each woman in her own right exemplified unusual fortitude, forbearance, capacity for austerity, selflessness, and surrender. For those who served in India, they manifested that rare ability to transcend the cultural boundaries of their origins and wholeheartedly remake themselves according to the ancient Indian ideals of sacrifice and selflessness. Taken together, their contribution to Vedanta in the East and the West continues to benefit each generation of spiritual aspirants. We are grateful to Linda Prugh, author of *Josephine MacLeod and Vivekananda's Mission* (see book review this issue) for offering an overview of each of these exemplary Western disciples of Vivekananda.

Between 1847 and 1867, five women were born in the West whose names would become well known in the annals of the Ramakrishna Order as devotees of Swami Vivekananda.

Christine Greenstidle (1866-1930), was the first of the five to hear Swami Vivekananda speak. Though she was to be among the well-known disciples of Vivekananda, there would be only about six periods in which she was actually in his company. However, the swami wrote dozens of letters to her.

Vivekananda spoke in Detroit on February 14, 1894. Christine and her friend Mary Funke were there, and she later wrote: "[When Vivekananda spoke, it] was the mind that made the first great appeal, that amazing mind!..." "...it was a mind so far transcending other minds, even of those who rank as geniuses..." "...Its ideas were so clear, so powerful, so transcendental that it seemed incredible that they could have emanated from the intellect of a limited human being."

Reading that Vivekananda would be with some students at Thousand Island Park in New York State, the summer of 1895, Christine and Mary boldly set out to journey there. When she met the swami, Christine blurted out: "We have come to you just as we would go to Jesus and ask him to teach us." She was initiated with some others the next day.

Christine wrote: "Only if one's mind were lifted to that high state of consciousness in which we lived for the time, could we hope to recapture the experience. We were filled with joy. We did not know that we were living in his radiance. On the wings of inspiration he carried us to the height which was his natural abode. He himself later said he was at his best at Thousand Islands."

In India, a monk once asked Christine: "How could you Western students understand Vedanta? To understand Vedanta, one must know Sanskrit; one must study all the commentaries of Shankara." Christine replied: "You do not know who taught us Vedanta. It was Vivekananda. He raised our minds to a very high plane."

In March, 1896, the swami was in Detroit. Christine recalled: "At this time the power had been transformed into a diviner radiance and a deeper compassion for the world which he was soon to leave. He rose and poured forth majestic truths in a voice which completed a beautiful harmony of appearance, voice, and message."

Christine saw Vivekananda twice between July 1899 and July 1900. The swami's letters to her reveal deep concern for her well being, knowing that he himself had only a short time to live. The first time they met he had asked Mary Funke if Christine was a pure soul. When she answered, "Yes, she is absolutely pure in heart," he had exclaimed: "I knew it. I felt it. I must have her for my work in Calcutta."

On July 6, 1901, he wrote to Christine: "I am small, very; but I know you are great and my faith is always in your true heart. I worry about everything except you. I have dedicated you to the Mother. She is your shield, your guide."

In December 1901, Christine's mother passed away. The swami wrote to her, enclosing a draft for $480, saying, "Do just as the way opens to you, and do not worry."

Christine arrived in Calcutta on April 7, 1902. Four weeks later Vivekananda sent her up to the Mayavati monastery in the Himalayas. On July 5 she received a cable that he had left his body on July 4. Christine wrote to Josephine MacLeod: "We would not have him suffering in body, tortured in mind – no, not

even for an hour would we. We would rather suffer the pains and bear the sense of loss."

Sister Christine lived for many years in Calcutta, teaching at Nivedita's school for girls. She returned to America in 1928, and passed in New York in 1930.

Sara Chapman Bull (1850-1911), was a widow when she met Swami Vivekananda in the spring of 1894. That summer they were both at the Greenacre Religious Conference in Eliot, Maine. It was here that the swami was able for the first time to teach both the philosophy and practice of Vedanta. He wanted to write on the subject, and he wanted to settle down and have regular classes. Sara invited the swami to be her guest in Cambridge, Mass. She had a large home, with a separate studio in which he would have perfect rest and freedom. In January, 1895, the swami's first lodging-classroom was set up at 54 West 33rd Street in New York City.

In March of 1896, Vivekananda was invited to speak at Harvard, where he had spoken in 1894. While in Cambridge he was Sara's guest, and students met with the swami there. He wrote to her October 18, 1896: "It is needless for me to state that you have my implicit confidence in all works in the U.S. And that [I] entrust everything there to you."

Sara Bull and her friend Josephine MacLeod wanted to travel to India. On July 10, 1897, Swami Vivekananda wrote: "Do come by all means, only you must remember this: The Europeans and the Hindus live as oil and water. If you mix with the English much here, you will have more comforts but see nothing of the Hindus as they are. Possibly I will not be able to eat with you, but I promise that I will travel to many places with you and do everything in my power to make your journey pleasant."

In January 1898, Sara Bull and Josephine MacLeod arrived in Calcutta. Their stay lasted almost a full year, half of which was spent on a pilgrimage to the Himalayas with Vivekananda and some monks. That spring the women and Margaret Noble (Sister Nivedita) lived in a dilapidated cottage on the grounds of Belur, a property recently purchased for a monastery. It was here that these three women forged the bonds that would unite them for the rest of their lives. Vivekananda came there mornings for tea and to talk about India. Writing to an American devotee, he declared: "These yanks can do anything, after the comforts of Boston and New York, to be quite content and happy with this wretched little house."

In the fall of 1899, Swami Vivekananda was the guest for ten weeks of Francis and Betty Leggett at their home, Ridgely, in New York. Nivedita and Sara Bull were among the guests. On November 5, 1899, the swami called Nivedita and Sara to him, placed his hands on their heads, and said: "I give you all that Ramakrishna gave to me. What came to me through a woman I give to you two women."

For the rest of Sara's life she helped to support Sister Nivedita in her work for a girls school. Sara passed January 18, 1911, with Nivedita at her side.

Josephine MacLeod (1858 to 1949) first heard Vivekananda speak on Tuesday, January 29, 1895. It was the second day of classes in his New York City headquarters. She later recalled: "He said something and instantly to me that was truth, and the second sentence he spoke was truth, and the third sentence was truth. From that moment life had a different import."

All her adult life Joe sought freedom. Because she valued freedom herself, one of the great gifts she gave Swami Vivekananda was freedom. When he stayed with her family Joe helped with arrangements. Later she wrote about hosting: "[One's guest] must be free to go or come; or stay, or do or not do – just let the mood be followed. It was that attitude in our family towards Swamiji that kept him with and near us. Days without speaking, days and nights continuous speaking! We followed his moods and kept ourselves busy in our own lives and happy when he wasn't about, so that there was no sort of weight put upon him."

Vivekananda himself spoke about Joe's effect on him in making things happen. On their way to London, aboard ship, the swami told Nivedita: "[Joe] is my good star. When she is with me, everything goes well." And from London he wrote to Joe: "The upshot of the whole thing is, there can be no work in London because you are not here. You seem to be my fate."

Joe MacLeod is known for having said that she was never Vivekananda's disciple; she was his friend. Perhaps she felt that a disciple's attitude toward one's guru necessarily implied responsibilities placed on the teacher. She never wanted "any sort of weight" to be put on him. However, he did give her a mantra at some point, and she said: "I can't do this." Then many years later, in India, she found that mantra welling up and repeating itself automatically.

In March 1902, Joe was at Belur Math visiting the swami. Later she wrote: "Vivekananda said, 'I shall never see forty.' I, knowing he was 39, said, 'But, Swami, Buddha did not do his great work until between 40 and 80.' He said, 'I delivered my message and I must go. The shadow of a big tree will not allow smaller trees to grow. I must go to make room.'"

In London on July 5, Joe received a cable announcing the swami's passing. She was shattered, and later wrote: "The devastation that seemed to fill my life made me weep for years and it was only after I read Maeterlinck who said, 'If you have been greatly influenced by anyone, prove it in your life and not by your tears,' that I never wept again but went back to America and tried to follow the traces of where Vivekananda had lived. Joe travelled to India many times for long stays. She passed

October 15, 1949 at the Vedanta Society in Hollywood.

Margaret Noble (Sister Nivedita) (1867-1911), first heard Vivekananda speak on a Sunday afternoon in November 1895 in London. Her reaction was that he said nothing new, but she went to his next lectures. The swami returned to London in April 1896 and she attended his classes and met Josephine MacLeod. Before the swami returned to India, she regarded him as her teacher. She wrote: "I saw that although he had a system of thought to offer, nothing in that system would claim him for a moment if he found that truth led elsewhere. And to the extent that this recognition implies, I became his disciple."

In the summer of 1897, when Margaret wrote to the swami, offering to go to India to teach, he asked that she stay in London. Then she wrote, saying that she wanted to go to India to learn. On July 29, 1897, he replied: "Let me tell you frankly that I am now convinced that you have a great future in the work for India. What was wanted was not a man but a woman, a real lioness to work for the Indians, women specially. You must think well before you plunge in, and after work, if you fail in this or get disgusted, on my part I promise you I will stand by you unto death whether you work for India or not, whether you give up Vedanta or remain in it."

In January, 1898, Margaret Noble arrived in Calcutta and was joined by Josephine MacLeod and Sara Bull. They met Sri Sarada Devi (known as Holy Mother), the spiritual consort of Sri Ramakrishna, and on March 25, Margaret received initiation and became known as Sister Nivedita (the Dedicated). Vivekananda, with other monks, led the women on a Himalayan pilgrimage.

In June, 1899, Swami Vivekananda, Swami Turiyananda, and Sister Nivedita sailed to England. It was a six-week journey, with daily conversations recorded in her diary and letters to friends. These records helped her immensely in writing her masterpiece, *The Master as I Saw Him*, published in 1910.

After the swami's passing, July 4, 1902, Nivedita wrote books, mentored young freedom workers, and kept the school for girls going with the help of Sister Christine. Writing to Joe MacLeod on April 29, 1903, she confided: "I sit alone, writing, and do none of the things I used to do. Christine is going to take up all the old plans. It [used to seem] I was 'the lioness born to work for India.' And now it seems to me that it was really Christine who was to do the things that He planned for me."

Sister Nivedita wrote the introduction to *The Complete Works of Swami Vivekananda*. One paragraph of that introduction gives the essence of the Vedanta that Vivekananda taught: "If the many and the One be indeed the same Reality, then it is not all modes of worship alone, but equally all modes of work, all modes of struggle, all modes of creation, which are paths of realization. No distinction, henceforth, between sacred and secular. To labor is to pray. To conquer is to renounce. Life is itself religion." In the fall of 1911, Sister Nivedita went to Darjeeling with friends, fell very ill, and passed on October 13.

Charlotte Sevier (1847-1930), and her husband, Capt. Harry Sevier, heard Swami Vivekananda speak in London in the spring of 1896. One day Harry Sevier asked Josephine MacLeod, "Is this young man what he seems to be?" She answered "Yes." Harry said, "Then we must follow him and find God!"

Within a short time, the swami agreed to go with them to Switzerland and Germany. In the cool Swiss alps Vivekananda meditated on establishing a Himalayan monastery. When they returned to England he stayed with the Seviers, and on October 28 wrote to a disciple in India: "Mr. and Mrs. Sevier are going to open an ashrama in the Himalayas near Almora." In December the swami and the Seviers left for India, along with Swamiji's stenographer, J. J. Goodwin.

In March 1899, a tea plantation was found in Mayavati for the monastery. Vivekananda declared: "Here it is hoped to keep Advaita free from all superstitions and weakening contaminations. Here will be taught and practiced nothing but the Doctrine of Unity, pure and simple, and though in entire sympathy with all other systems [of philosophy], this Ashrama is dedicated to Advaita and Advaita alone."

The swami envisioned that in this climate, the ashrama, at 7,000 feet, would be livable for Westerners and Easterners. Unfortunately, Harry Sevier suffered from neuralgia and died of cystitis in October of 1900. Swami Vivekananda travelled to visit Mother Sevier, and stayed at Mayavati for two weeks in January 1901. There he wrote: "Mayavati is very, very beautiful, and they have made it simply exquisite. It is a huge place several acres in area and is very well kept."

The editorial offices of Prabuddha Bharata, an English journal of the Ramakrishna Order, were established at Mayavati, and Mother Sevier helped with its editing and wrote numerous articles. She also contributed to the first edition of *The Life of Swami Vivekananda*.

Once Josephine MacLeod, while visiting Mayavati, asked Charlotte, "Don't you ever get bored?" Charlotte answered: "I think of Swamiji when I feel time heavy on me." In April 1916, Charlotte Sevier returned to England. She passed on October 20, 1930. [see Book Review, Mother of Mayavati]

Linda Prugh is a longtime member of the Vedanta Society of Kansas City, and currently serves as its secretary. She is a former English teacher and has an M.A. in Reading Education. She is the author of *Josephine MacLeod and Vivekananda's Mission*, and has contributed articles to Vedanta journals over the last 30 years. She has been active on the Greater Kansas City Interfaith Council since 2005.

THE DEDICATED ONE
The Faith and Devotion of Sister Nivedita

*When God calls her, let her go;
she will spread her wings.
She will do great things.*

These were the prophetic words spoken to his wife by Samuel Richmond Noble, an Irish Protestant minister, before his premature death at the age of thirty-four. The reference was to his daughter, Margaret Elizabeth Noble, who was born on October 28, 1867. The Noble family had taken an active part in the Irish freedom movement, so the spirit of freedom was in Margaret's blood. On completion of her formal education, she took to teaching and founded a school called the Ruskin School in Wimbledon. She adopted the method of teaching developed by Pestalozzi and Froebel. She also became secretary of the Sesame Club, where the intellectual elite of the day, including Bernard Shaw and T. H. Huxley, held discussions on a variety of topics.

Margaret was a devout Christian, but her spirit was restless. She turned to the study of Buddhism but found no answer to her questions and doubts. She was ever in search of that Light and Truth which lies beyond the limits set by religious doctrines. The turning point in her life came in November, 1895.

Finding Her Master

Swami Vivekananda visited England in the second half of that year, after a whirlwind tour of America following his success at the Parliament of Religions in Chicago in 1893. His fame had already spread, for he had taken America by storm via his convincing eloquence and nondual message. The "cyclonic monk," as he was called in the States, came to be known as the Hindu Yogi in England. It was in the drawing room of lady Isabel Margesson, an English devotee, where Margaret met Swami Vivekananda. At first she was impressed by his magnetic personality, but initially his views made no impact on her. During his second visit in 1896, however, his message in its validity, relevance, and profundity came home to her. Margaret had found her Master and willingly became a "convert." As K. R. Srinivasa Iyengar was later to write, "*As an angler of souls, Vivekananda's most valuable catch was Miss Margaret Noble.*"

Call to Service

Ireland and Calcutta were world's apart, so when Margaret expressed her desire to go to India, Vivekananda warned her against the many difficulties and obstacles she would have to reckon with. The appalling condition of the people of India, their poverty, ignorance, disease, superstition, their antiquated customs and conventions, the inhospitable climate, the hostile attitude of her own people in India, and also the suspicion and opposition of the Orthodox natives in India to foreigners. If she chose to come in spite of these odds, however, he gave her his assurance that he would "*stand by her unto death.*" As Sri Ramakrishna had said, "*The tusks of the elephant come out, but never go back, so are the words of an honest man never to be retracted.*" Margaret did not waver in her decision to make India her home and place of service. She departed and reached Calcutta on January 28, 1898.

In India

Three significant events took place following her arrival. On March 11, Vivekananda introduced her to the people of Calcutta at a public meeting, describing her as "*a gift of England to India.*" On March 17, she received the blessing of Mother Saradamani, Sri Ramakrishna's spiritual consort. On March 25, she consecrated her life to the service of God and Mother India. Vivekananda gave her the name Nivedita, which means one who has dedicated oneself or made an offering of oneself to God. Margaret's father's words had come true.

In the summer of 1898, Vivekananda took Mrs. Sara Bull and Miss Josephine Macleod, two American disciples, Nivedita, and a few others on a tour of the Himalayas and other places of historical and cultural interest in North India, and enlightened them on the different aspects of Indian history and culture in order to prepare them for their life's mission. On her return from the instructional tour, Nivedita subjected herself to a rigorous discipline of mind and body, studying the Gita, practicing meditation, and adapting herself to a simple Indian lifestyle. In this

period of training she did not lose sight of the driving force which brought her from Ireland, namely service to India.

In 1898 she started a school for girls and the inauguration was presided over by Holy Mother. Education was imparted to the children and their mothers, who were taught to read, write, sew, paint, etc. *"The hands that serve are better than the lips that pray,"* she quoted, following the directives of her Master. Nara seva is Narayana seva (service of God in mankind).

In 1899, plague broke out in Calcutta, and Nivedita organized a group of young people to tend the afflicted. She set a personal example of manual service for others to follow. She also visited England and America to organize funds for her work, and also to enlighten the Western world on India and her problems. Returning in 1902, she made house No. 17 on Bosepara Lane in Calcutta her headquarters. It was her home, school, and her nucleus of intellectual, spiritual, and social service activity.

Participation in India's Independence

After Vivekananda's passing in 1902, Nivedita felt that she could not confine her work only to the spiritual field and the education of girls. Her innate spirit of freedom would not let her be a passive spectator of India suffering under foreign rule. She plunged into the Indian National movement and identified herself with the Indian cause for Independence, traveling extensively and exhorting the Indians to fight for emancipation. The English Raj was embarrassed but could do nothing about it. And when the public singing of Bande Mataram was banned, she had the courage to have it sung at her school prayer meetings.

The development of art and science engaged her attention. She evinced interest in the revival of ancient Indian art and appealed to artists to concern themselves with Indian life and themes. She was a source of inspiration and encouragement to Jagdish Chandra Bose as well, and helped him in the publication of his books and articles. She worked tirelessly for women's upliftment, and advised them to follow their tradition and not to be carried away by the newfangled ways of the West.

Nivedita considered herself primarily as a child and servant of Mother India. Her concern was for the unity of India. She told the youth, *"It is true that in India, we have many races, many religions, and many kinds of social conditions, but that does not mean that all cannot be united into one."* Nivedita was a many-sided personality — a spiritual seeker, devotee, educationist, freedom fighter, social worker, and a savant. She belongs to that august line of distinguished women from the West such as Madeline Slade (Mira Behn), Annie Besant, Mrs. Welthy Fisher, Mother Teresa, and Ida Scudder, who made India their home and field of activity, not out of necessity, but out of choice and inner compulsion and commitment.

On October 7, 1911, Sister Nivedita fashioned her will, leaving all her possessions and writings in the Custody of Trustees of the Belur Math to be used for her school, The Ramakrishna Sarada Mission Sister Nivedita Girl's School. She passed away at Darjeeling at sunrise on October 13, 1911.

The late S. Jagadisan was a Professor of English at Presidency College (a prestigious post graduate institution in India) in Chennai, India. His articles on a variety of subjects include Swami Vivekananda and Sri Ramakrishna.

The Open Space Beyond Religion

Open Space is the placeless place
where all prayers and elevated intentions come to full fruition.
Open Space is the one taste that pervades all beings, all events.

Open Space is not space.
Open Space is not something open or closed.
Open Space does not have any form.
Open Space is not formlessness.
One cannot describe Open Space by saying what it is not.
There is no way to describe what already is.

There is nothing inside Open Space, there is nothing outside it.
But Open Space is a mother nursing her child.
Open Space is a child's game.
Open Space is the justice, the beauty, the mercy,
the transparent light that manifests as cosmos.
Open Space is plenitude.
Everything that spiritual traditions long for,
supplicate for, envision,
and have envisioned profoundly and authentically
from the very beginning of consciousness,
all this richness is the plenitude of Open Space.

Open Space is what is hearing at this moment.
Open Space is the temporality that we identify as this moment.
Open Space is infinitely articulate.
It speaks through every possible language.
It speaks through the nonverbal gestures of our lives.
Its perfect silence is perfect speech.
Its perfect speech is perfect silence.

A profusion, a cascade of names are indicating Open Space.
Here are some of the names of Open Space:
microphone, floor, hands, eyes,
air, chandelier, Chicago, planet Earth.

Open Space is sublime reticence.
Not a single explanation, not a single statement
issues from Open Space.
Words cease to be words for Open Space.
Sounds cease to be sounds,
tastes cease to be tastes, for Open Space.
We lose ourselves in order to find ourselves as Open Space.

— Lex Hixon, speaking as the "Open Space Beyond Religion" (the only name he had written on his name-tag) at the second Parliament of the World's Religions, September, 1993, Chicago, Illinois.

Lex Hixon, Babaji Bob Kindler, Bhavatarini Ma, and students at SRV National, Greenville, New York.

THE INVISIBLE THREAD
Weaving A Personal Journey

Go forth, little one, and meet life
Strong in the strength of freedom from self.
The strength of purity,
The strength of love.
    ---- from Child Heart by Sister Nivedita

Two unique Western women disciples of Swami Vivekananda went on to play a significant role in India. Sister Nivedita, from England, and Sister Christine, from America, followed Swamiji to India for his work of education, especially for women. Sister Christine's work was more in the background, unheralded, and chiefly focused on the education of women. This article, however, concentrates mainly on Sister Nivedita whose 150th birth anniversary we are celebrating this year.

Nivedita's efforts and contributions in the field of education, science, literature, art, history, and politics in India were immense. She has been diversely characterized as a blazing flame, goddess, nationalist, patriot, etc., but perhaps the best epithet that she has received is that of a being who breathed the breath of life into India's old dry bones to create the country anew, and with sacrifice and renunciation as its mantra. This was perhaps the work for which she was commissioned. One is reminded of the wrath of Shiva at the yagna of Daksha and the insult of Sati therein, which impelled him to tear a lock of matted hair from his head in rage and hurl it on the ground. From it emerged Kali who then destroyed Daksha's yagna, and Daksha himself. Sister Nivedita is perhaps one such lock of matted hair, which destroyed the yagna of colonialism in India that had already begun to crumble due to the work of great souls like her at the turn of the 20th century in Calcutta, and India.

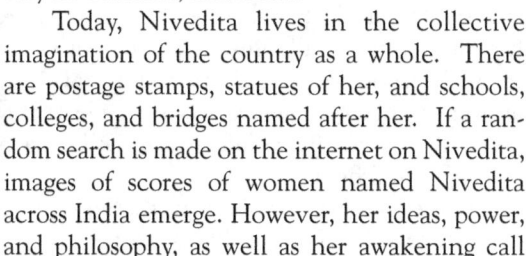

Today, Nivedita lives in the collective imagination of the country as a whole. There are postage stamps, statues of her, and schools, colleges, and bridges named after her. If a random search is made on the internet on Nivedita, images of scores of women named Nivedita across India emerge. However, her ideas, power, and philosophy, as well as her awakening call appears to be all but invisible. It flows like the mythical river *Saraswati*, in hidden undercurrents. When working for the underprivileged in India today, among those whom she had fully dedicated herself, realization dawns that she still lives as a palpable presence.

Education in India — An Unfinished Agenda

Sister Nivedita's educational ideal was cosmopolitan, wherein all cultures, languages, and religions are so many different scripts through which inner freedom is expressing itself. It was her cosmopolitanism which allowed her to integrate with the caste-ridden, superstitious, and insular world of the women of north Calcutta, and subsequently with the whole of India. Her activities were focused on India, for that was, as per her own realization, the work for which Swamiji dedicated her. In light of this realization, and to pursue diverse activities in all social fields, she had to make the most painful decision of formally disassociating from the Ramakrishna Mission. She felt that raising the masses and women of India, an ideal precious to Swamiji, could best be achieved through this more independent course. For Swamiji, raising the women and masses was vital not only for India, but crucial for the world too, for India was to make a vital contribution to the grand symphony of global civilization. Following the lead of her guru, they both began to deliver to the world a superlative message of tolerance and acceptance, of renunciation and service, of peace and harmony, of unity in diversity, and the oneness of all existence. Only a vibrant, socially strong India, imbued with this integrated vision, would convey this exceptional message to the world.

Today, much still remains to be done in India in the field of education of the masses, and of women. More than 300 million people in the country remain illiterate, and the situation is much graver for women. Many of those who are literate are really functionally illiterate. The government introduced the Right to Education Act in 2009, which provides free and compulsory education for all children in the age group of six to fourteen years as a Fundamental Right. Although India has one of the largest welfare schemes for education, it faces multiple challenges in implementation ranging from difficult teacher-student ratio, teacher absenteeism, lack of infrastructure, and lack of resources. More than 8 million children in the age group 6-14 remain out of school, and there's a shortage of more than 0.5 million teachers country-wide. Some studies point out that 76% of students do not make it to a higher education system. 40% of children in standard 3 cannot recognize numbers up to 100. 52% of children in standard 5 cannot read a standard 2 text. The immense desire to learn remains unfulfilled and not sufficiently addressed. The situation is acute amidst the urban squalor and among the migrant population in mega cities like Delhi.

Perhaps Sister Nivedita's prescription in this regard both explains the situation and provides a direction. Like her guru, Vivekananda, she stressed that we have to build up this idea of giving education to the people as our sacred duty, it being one of

> "Unless we strive for truth because we love it and strive to attain it; unless we learn to live and rejoice in the life of thought, great things of the heart and intellect will close their doors to us. A nation stands or falls in the long run by the number of such souls that it is capable of producing out of the rank and file of ordinary people."

the main elements that would resurrect Indian civilization. As an extension of the idea of giving alms intrinsic in our civilization, she cited the unfortunate fact that in most Western countries, it is required that every young man, when his education is complete, shall give three, four, or five years to military service, and to remain for the rest of his life ready at any moment to join in the armed defense of his country. In like fashion, and much more worthy, she opined that India needed to organize the army of education. Every student, when his or her education was completed, should be called upon to give three years to the betterment of the people. It would, of course, be understood, that just as the only son of a widow in the West gets excused from military service, so one whose earnings are absolutely necessary to others he or she supports must also be excused this mandatory educational service. The community, on the other hand, would reciprocate and maintain the student living amongst them as a schoolmaster.

In this way, the duty of teaching on one hand, and the duty of maintaining on the other, would combine to create the perfect social unit — the result being that in due course of time the greater masses of people might be swept into this widening circle of enlightened articulation. The educational process has to be self-supporting and self-propagating. "Alms to the teacher" and "knowledge to the people" must be converse truths, both maintained at one and the same time. Unfortunately, no government organization ever arranges for a wise scheme like this, one that brings education to all, equally. Only through a shared common cause among the people and the students can this plan be made a reality.

The Method of Education

As Vivekananda often reiterated, each soul is potentially divine, and the goal is that each person must consciously seek that divinity by carving out a road to the infinite and developing an independent path for himself, so to say. The preceptor can only provide suggestions and possible directions, but the struggle is one's own. Each being has to think her own thoughts, speak her own words, and stand on her own legs. This inherent uniqueness applied to the process of acquiring knowledge demands a special vibrancy in the educational process, and Sister Nivedita had this quality in abundance.

The holistic education developed by Nivedita, rooted in the culture of her students, is a direct pointer of how one needs to proceed. Holistic growth in contrast to "one-sided education," replete with empathy for all, as well as a consuming interest for all streams of knowledge — and at the same time a bulldog-like intensity in fastening on to one's own ideals — this is the higher global ideal introduced by Sri Ramakrishna. It is meant to broaden out to include all other forms, but without losing the intensity and depth of that singular endeavor which is one's own.

Concretely, around education, Sister Nivedita delineated three chronologically distinct elements which are as vital today as they were in her time. They were:

a) Train the human mind to be an instrument of knowledge, and focus its powers to benefit others.

b) Gather a copious fund of ideas and concepts common to society as a whole, and impart them to every individual.

c) Prepare this special message for the individual, and thereby enhance his/her unique chance of contributing to the educational riches of humanity.

For her, all educational endeavors need to weave their respective patterns around these elements, thereby assisting in manifesting the immense potentialities coiled in the mind of students.

Further, there was another element of educational effort that she favored, relative to all kinds of external social effort for spiritual practitioners or seekers. This was the realm of Karma Yoga — work as an offering to the Infinite, and also as a purificatory means of self-abnegation. This would effectively erase the small "I" in order to realize the larger "I." For Nivedita, as well as for Sister Christine, this well-developed Vedic Yoga was implicit, for their lives were blazing fires which only burnt in order to give warmth to others. The school that Nivedita started, and they operated together, is still standing tall today, and has played a crucially important role in the establishment of the great order of nuns of the Ramakrishna tradition.

Nivedita's Aim for Education

To Sister Nivedita, the consummate end of education is cosmopolitan and universal for all times and all climes. Here, all humanity is in oneness. For her, by the attainment of universality does education stand either justified or condemned. However, she stressed that the ideals presented must always be clothed in a form evolved by our own past; for imagination to be effective it must be based on our heroic literature. Hope, also, to have any worth at all, must be woven out of our human history. In all learning we should attempt to give knowledge only in answer to sincere enquiry. This is the ideal. If we could attain it perfectly, every child would grow up to be a genius in his or her own right and field.

However, curiosity about truth can only grow within one's perceived world. The familiar is not the goal; specialized knowledge is the goal, and trained faculties are the aim. Inside of this goal, universality is the aim, where all educated persons of the world can meet, understand, and enjoy each other's association. To grow into the universal mindset is an uphill task, no doubt, and no shortcuts are available for it. Souls have to grow via knowledge — from what is familiar to what seems unfamiliar.

> "....mere telling is not teaching. To achieve a balance between mere information and actual learning is often a great struggle. According to Nivedita, right training is the result of right will, and it cannot be evoked by mere words of command."

Nivedita avowed that it would be a sin to bring up an Indian child on anything but the *Mahabharata*. An Indian child could better appreciate the beauty of the truthfulness of a being such as Yudhishthira, common to his own culture and scriptures, but may not identify at all with, say, the poetry of Homer. Further, she reiterated that mere telling is not teaching. To achieve a balance between mere information and actual learning is often a great struggle. According to Nivedita, right training is the result of right will, and it cannot be evoked by mere words of command.

To Nivedita there is another facet of education: the hunger for the good of others as an end in itself. In this sense a child's center of gravity must lie for them outside the family. Mutual aid, co-operation, and self-organized unselfishness is to be the motto. There is nothing so belittling to the human soul as the acquisition of knowledge for the sake of worldly reward. There is nothing so degrading to a nation as coming to look upon the life of the mind as a means for bread-winning. Unless we strive for truth because we love it and strive to attain it; unless we learn to live and rejoice in the life of thought, great things of the heart and intellect will close their doors to us. A nation stands or falls in the long run by the number of such souls that it is capable of producing out of the rank and file of ordinary people.

Our Experience

As seekers on the spiritual path one is always expecting signs, be it more calmness and peace, or visions and abilities, or looking for expansion and attaining deeper love. But the Divine is perhaps not interested in giving any of these, and instead through a simple course of events puts the traveler on a different and new path which had not been envisioned before.

Our forays into the field of education started as if by chance. One cold, foggy winter night way back in 2002 we were forced into the world of a frail three or four-year-old under-privileged girl, running in the middle of the road desperately trying to search for her mother, whose whereabouts she vaguely knew to be working in some high-rise apartment. She knew not which apartment her mother worked, and on being asked she, with great trust, led us to her home, which was a locked door in the urban village – Chilla in east Delhi – adjoining a colony of high rise apartments. We did as much as we could do then, but this emotionally overpowering incident forced us, as it were, into initiating our small endeavor with children in the village. Fourteen years have passed and the small lamp of our sacrifice that was lit that night still burns in front of the altar.

By February 2003, on the auspicious day of Saraswati puja, we rented a small 10 ft x 10 ft room amongst the single-room quarters of migrant workers in the village with the help of a housemaid. Students of all ages poured in, mostly first generation learners. Due to the constraints of space the limit has been kept at 30 students. Some of them were already enrolled in the neighborhood government school, and the first task was to get all children coming to the class registered in those public schools. The work is in the nature of after-school instructional and tutorial classes for mostly first generation learners, children who are not privileged to access the available educational facilities. The basic emphasis during these ensuing 14 years has been to work on languages, both Hindi and English, mathematics,

geography, and history. Our emphasis has leaned towards making the young students be inspired to learn, rather than merely collect information and facts. Self-study and peer study circles are encouraged. Some of the students who started the journey with us are today pursuing higher studies, and doing graduate courses.

The platform is for all sincere students, and many volunteers have joined us for various periods of time, sharing their experience of music, arts (painting, drawing, and craft), storytelling, articulation, and expression exercises, and also teaching regular school subjects. The center is wholly supported by our personal resources, but people have been contributing funds off and on. We have received constant blessings from many revered practitioners of the Ramakrishna-Vivekananda tradition. It is blissful to see the senior students pursuing graduation, and initiating their own endeavors to help other children in need.

Interestingly, when domestic and professional reasons forced us recently to be less active participants, threatening closure of the center, the senior girls readily took over the command, emerging from the background as a solid force. This wholly unimagined and unplanned development had striking resemblances with the experience and practice of Nivedita's school, where senior students graduated to teaching.

The Presence of the Great Master

One decision we have consciously and deliberately taken has been to weave our activities around Sri Ramakrishna and the spiritual life that he lived. His inclusive God-centered path, celebrating the spiritual realization of all religions through different creeds, is an incomparable ideal that we keep. We came to real-

ize later that this is one issue which was also deliberated by Nivedita, and kept as a cornerstone in her educational endeavors. It was a departure from the secular trend of education up to her time, and even now. Swami Vivekananda, too, had expressed and encouraged this direction, saying that it is reasonable and possible to go beyond sects through a sect.

Therefore, we celebrate the festivals of all religions. As Sister Nivedita has said, *"I would like to teach everyone the greatest respect for everyone else's creed."*

Classes begin and end with chanting and prayers. Rallying around Sri Ramakrishna and Sri Sarada Devi's name has made us introduce concepts of universalism, expansion, selfless activity, renunciation, and service as the basis for our curriculum. The class concludes with chanting universal prayers seeking peace squalor rooms measuring 9 ft. by 10 ft. are entire households, it is a constant fight to train the mind and cultivate beneficial occupations. The bane of television and popular movie cultures dominate instead. Be that as it may, the struggle of minds, young and old, to rise against all these odds can be an enriching experience. All who have volunteered at our small educational habitat have experienced the infectious vibrancy of both the work and the place.

When we look into our experience and read about Sister Nivedita's initial efforts of establishing her school, we realize that there are uncanny similarities in the methods, aims, ideals, and events. The parallels make us feel that it is her work that we are made to carry out in our own small and humble way. She lives on and toils for the people of India, her chosen country.

> "Classes begin and end with chanting and prayers. Rallying around Sri Ramakrishna and Sri Sarada Devi's name has made us introduce concepts of universalism, expansion, selfless activity, renunciation, and service as the basis for our curriculum. Like her guru, Swami Vivekananda, Sister Nivedita stressed that any kind of studious engagement requires one particular dynamic force, that of character: *Yato Dharmastato Jayah* — "Where there is Dharma there is victory.""

and happiness for all, followed by a short guided meditation. Like her guru, Swami Vivekananda, Sister Nivedita stressed that any kind of studious engagement requires one particular dynamic force, that of character: *Yato Dharmastato Jayah* — *"Where there is Dharma there is victory."* This is true for both the teacher and the taught. Nivedita's stress on first making a fine character was so firm that she could say, *"Tell me your hobbies and I will tell you what sort of citizen you will make."* Because, in migrant urban We pray that we may acquire even a particle of her spirit and also be an offering to her God – "This, the desire to serve, the longing to better conditions, to advance our fellows, to lift the whole, is the real religion of the present day. Everything else is doctrine, opinion, theory." In this way she epitomizes the benediction conferred on her by the great Swami Vivekananda:

**Be thou to India's future son
The mistress, servant, friend in one.**

Sindhu and Joyesh are a couple based in Delhi. Sindhu is a high school teacher and Joyesh is a geologist by profession. Both are practitioners in the Sarada Ramakrishna tradition for more than 15 years.

THE VOICE OF THE MOTHER

by Sister Nivedita

Arise, My child, and go forth a man!
Bear manfully what is thy lot to bear;
that which comes to thy hand to be done,
do with full strength and fear not.
Forget not that I, the giver of manhood,
the giver of womanhood, the holder of victory,
am thy Mother.

Think not life is serious!
What is destiny but thy Mother's play?
Come, be My playfellow awhile —
meet all happenings merrily.
Murmurest thou of need of purpose?
Think'st thou the ball is purposeless,
with which the Mother plays?
Know'st thou not that Her toy is a thunderbolt,
charged with power to shatter the worlds,
at the turn of Her wrist?
Ask not of plans. Needs the arrow any plan
when it is loosed from the bow? Such art thou.
When the life is lived, the plan will stand revealed.
Till then, O child of time, know nothing!
My sport is unerring.
For that alone set forth on the day's journey.
Think it was for My pleasure
thou camest forth into the world,
and for that again, when night falls,
and My desire is accomplished,
I shall withdraw thee to My rest.
Ask nothing. Seek nothing. Plan nothing.
Let My will flow through thee,
as the ocean through an empty shell.
But this thing understand.
Not one movement shall be in vain.
Not one effort shall fail at last.
The dream shall be less, not greater, than the deed.
Thou shalt go here or there for some petty reason,
and thy going shall subserve great ends.
Thou shalt meet and speak with many,
but some few shall be Mine from the beginning.
With these thou shall exchange a secret sign,
and they shall follow with thee.
And that sign?

Deep in the heart of hearts of Mine own
flashes the sacrificial knife of Kali.
Worshippers of the Mother are they from their birth
in Her incarnation of the sword.
Lovers of death are they — not lovers of life —
and of storm and stress.
Such shall come to thee with torch unlit for fire.
My voice cries out over the teeming earth for lives,
for the lives and blood of the crowned kings of men.

Remember that I Who cry
have shown also the way to answer.
For of every kind has the mother been the first,
for protection of her flock, to leap to death.
Religion, called by whatever name,
has been ever the love of death.
But today the flame of renunciation
shall be lighted in My lands
and consume men with a passion
beyond control of thought.
Then shall My people thirst for self-sacrifice
as others for enjoyment.
Then shall labour and suffering and service
be counted sweet instead of bitter.
For this age is great in time, and I, even I, Kali,
am the Mother of the nations.
Shrink not from defeat, embrace despair.
Pain is not different from pleasure, if I will both.
Rejoice therefore, when thou comest
to the place of tears, and see Me smile.
At such spots do I keep My tryst with men,
and fold them deep into My heart.
Uproot every interest that would conflict with Mine.
Neither love, nor friendship, nor comfort, nor home,
may make its voice heard when I speak.
Pass from a palace to plunge into the ocean of terror -
from the chamber of ease to stand guard in a burning city.
Know that as the one is unreal, so also is the other.
Meet fate with a smile.
Look for no mercy for thyself,
and I shall make thee bearer
of great vessels of mercy to others.
Accept bravely thine own darkness
and thy lamp shall cheer many.
Fulfill gladly the meanest service,
and leave high places unsought.
Be steadfast in the toil I set thee.
Weave well the warp into the woof.
Shrink from no demand that the task makes on thee.
Feel no responsibility. Ask for no reward.
Strong, fearless, resolute — when the sun sets,
and the game is done, thou shalt know well,
little one, that I, Kali, the giver of manhood,
the giver of womanhood,
and the withholder of victory, am thy Mother.

≈ VEDANTA 101 ≈
Vivarta & Viveka: False Superimposition and its Removal

In countless ways, illumined beings throughout the ages have said that we have within ourselves the Source of what we seek. Although this short essay is directed toward the spiritual seeker, this revelation of the illumined applies equally to everyone. Swami Vivekananda took great pains when he taught in the West during the late 1800's to explain how every action – good, bad, and mixed – is motivated by the desire for Freedom, to be without boundaries. One can prove this with a little contemplation. Boundaries, here, are anything that limits one's ability to exist in a state of ceaseless satisfaction, or peace. Such a state is synonymous with unending Joy, or Bliss *(Ananda)*. The spiritual aspirant will immediately recognize that, yes, the senses do not give accurate information or permanent pleasure, the body gets diseases and finally dies, its energy is limited, and the mind is also limited. There is no permanent or unending happiness or freedom in the psycho-physical being.

So, the more pertinent question is, from where does this desire for Freedom come? The Seers of India tell us that we cannot imagine something that is unknown to us. This impulse of freedom keeps showing up in our actions and desires because our own nature is boundless Freedom and Bliss. But if it is our nature, where is It? A better question would be, "Where is It not?"

The ancient Seers realized *Brahman,* the ultimate Reality, also called indivisible Existence, Knowledge, Bliss/Freedom, or *Sat-Chit-Ananda.* Along the way to this realization they transcended body, energy, mind, intellect, and the separate I-sense until the individual self finally merged with the Indivisible Self/Brahman. Vedantists will recognize these as the five *koshas*, or coverings over the Supreme Self. But what is important here is the idea of transcending these coverings. Religions and philosophies concerned with spiritual union will name and organize these coverings variously. The point remains that the state of indivisible Oneness is ever-present, but apparently covered up, and this principle is called *vivarta* in *Sanskrit.*

In English, vivarta is often translated as "false-superimposition." "Superimposition" means that something is superimposed over something else. For instance, mountains or buildings are superimposed over the horizon. The shadow of the Earth and the light of the Sun are superimposed over the moon causing it to appear large or small. The word "false" in the definition, means that we should not to be fooled by these appearances, but always see through them to the truth. The moon is always full, never half or quarter, etc. The horizon is actually formless, not jagged or shaped in any way. These are tangible examples; they show how our eyes can deceive us into thinking that something that is formless has a form, or, in the case of the moon, appears completely other than it really is.

Yet, the Seers have in mind something more subtle and rudimentary than those outer examples. They want us to understand that the origin of all superimpositions lies in and with the mind; from the very start we are superimposing concepts, names, and forms over formless Reality as soon as the mind breaks into thought, or Consciousness breaks into waves or vibrations. They explain this with the "snake in the rope" teaching: In the fading light of dusk, a person sees a snake in the road and reacts with fear. Gathering courage, they investigate that apparent snake and discover that it is actually a rope, thus finding that the vision of the snake was a product of their own mental projection only. Unlike the other examples that have a sensory basis, the snake was never actually present, was always and ever only a rope.

The snake stands for the world, i.e., all forms, ideational or atomic, and the rope stands for formless Reality. The seers have realized that one's own Self is formless Reality and ever Free. Vedanta and Yoga explain that through the power of cosmic and collective mind combined with desire for experiences, the individual mind projects phenomena over the indivisible Self, and then identifies with them. One's "I" gets falsely identified with body, energy, mind, intellect, and ego, as well as worlds, objects, desires and actions. However, this mistake does not change one's nature as being ever-Free, never bound. And this is why these beings keep trying to "get" that freedom back via experiences with all those coverings and objects.

The teaching of *vivarta* confirms for the spiritual aspirant where the longing for freedom arises, and gives us a word to describe the fact that form covers formlessness, limits cover the Limitless, action covers the natural state of Inaction, experiences cover the Experiencer, and so forth. Recognizing and understanding *vivarta* reveals the need to follow spiritual disciplines under the guidance of an illumined teacher to see through and transcend superimpositions.

Vivarta, if understood arightly, should also lead to the practice of spiritual disciplines, *sadhana.* It is closely aligned in Vedanta and other *darshanas* with *viveka,* the ability to discriminate between what is actual and what is illusory. It is to *"separate the wheat from the chaff,"* as Jesus explained it. The great swami mentioned in this essay perceived it to be the consummate practice in this age, being so enamored of it that he even took it as his name.

The chart on the facing page takes us deeper into the *vivarta/viveka* connection, revealing as it does how illusory coverings show up in us at the time of our birth in the body, hamper us in our attempts to meditate beyond all sheaths and coverings, and even insinuate themselves in and over such potentially sweet and benefical fields as the *Yoga* of Devotion, called *Bhakti.* The great seers who have visited this world advise the practice of the eight-limbed Yoga, the study of the revealed scriptures under the guidance of an authentic teacher (guru), and the dissolution of all desires of the mind by such sure and certain purifications.

Cutting Through Clouds of False Superimposition
The Indispensable Role of *Viveka* in Spiritual Life

"The appearance of the world, Oh Rama, is due to its being experienced through hundreds of births devoid of yogic discrimination. The discriminating soul will pass beyond mere enjoyments, then, and secure these three great attainments — The Knowledge of Truth, The Dissolution of the Mind, and The Effacement of Desires." Lord Vasishtha

Knowledge of Truth → Study of the scriptures is the means to Knowledge of Truth

Practice of Yoga is the means to Dissolution of Mind ← Dissolution of Mind

Effacement of Desires → Production of positive impressions is the means to effacement of latent impressions

Viveka at Birth

"The primary disease of the mind is the desire for rebirth. The secondary disease of the mind is reincarnation devoid of discriminative wisdom. From its absence comes lack of control of the senses and the inability to quell desires." Lord Vasishtha

Viveka of Bhakti

"The failure to implement Viveka into the path of Bhakti leads to worship of the ego rather than authentic Love of God. The outcome is preoccupation with surface practices like asana, and affectatious singing and dancing." Babaji Bob Kindler

Viveka in Meditation

"Sure knowledge of Brahman is gained by meditation upon correct teachings given by the illumined guru, and never through sacred ablutions, almsgiving, or hundreds of breathing exercises." Shankara

"That one attains to perfection who, restraining the mind and the senses via discrimination, directs all his organs along the path of dharmic works." Sri Krishna

Viveka in Karma/Activity

"The sterling virtue of discriminative restraint relies upon higher Knowledge, and that noble Wisdom depends upon this selfsame virtue — even as the lake and the lotus thrive upon one another. Through such rare and incomparable practice are the fetters of the heart severed, just like the threads running through a lotus when its stalk is cut." Lord Vasishtha in Jivan Mukti Viveka

Chart by Babaji Bob Kindler   Property of SRV Associations

Wisdom Facets From the Gem of Truth

Sri Ramakrishna

Holy Mother, Sri Sarada Devi

Real Gold, Not Fool's Gold.

"I ask people to live in the world after the awakening of their spiritual consciousness. After extracting gold from the earth through hard labor, a man may keep it buried underground or under water. The gold will not be affected."

(Gospel of Sri Ramakrishna)

"I Am Alone"

"To live in the world in a detached spirit is very difficult. By merely saying so one cannot be a King Janaka. How much austerity Janaka practiced. How long he remained still in one position. You do not have to practice such extreme disciplines, but you need to perform sadhana. You must live in solitude for a year, six months, three months, or even one month. You can then live in the world as a householder after attaining divine wisdom and love in solitude."

(Gospel of Sri Ramakrishna)

The Conundrum of Consciousness

"As a result of discrimination that Brahman alone is real and the world illusory, the aspirant goes into samadhi. For him, the forms and attributes of God disappear altogether. Then he does not feel God to be a person. He cannot describe in words what God is. And who will describe it? He who is to describe does not exist; he no longer finds his 'I,' To such a person God is attributeless. In that state God is experienced only as Consciousness, by man's inmost consciousness. He cannot be comprehended by mind and intelligence."

(Gospel of Sri Ramakrishna)

Why Cry Only One Tear for God?

"I used to weep so bitterly with the name of Divine Mother on my lips that people would stand in a row watching me."

(Gospel of Sri Ramakrishna)

Brahman Expressing Through Nature

"He, the Breath of the Universe, is singing His own praise, and you are hearing that eternal song through things that will come to an end. The trees, the birds, the hills, and all are singing praise to the Lord. The Banyan at Dakshineswar sings of Kali, to be sure, and blessed is he who has ears to hear it."

(From a letter to Nivedita included in the book, Eternal Mother)

Incomparable Doings of the Lord

"It gives me such delight to learn that you are speaking of Dhruva, Savitri, Sita, Rama, and so on, there. The accounts of their holy lives are better than all the vain talk of the world, I am sure. Oh! How beautiful are the Name and doings of the Lord!"

(ibid,, Eternal Mother)

The Great Master's Pure Love

"Early on, Sri Ramakrishna installed a pitcher of bliss in my very heart. And I became full of that Bliss. How profound was his love for me. When I used to reside in his room in Dakshineswar, all through the night he would be drowned either in samadhi, or would keep me drowned in talks on God."

(Sri Sarada Devi, the Great Wonder)

Ready or Not, Here They Come!

"Yogin Ma: "Look at the Master's disciples. Each one of them is a spiritual giant. But what about your disciples, Mother?"

Holy Mother: "Is it to be wondered at? He picked up the best types, and with what care he selected them! And towards me he has pushed all this small fry, coming in their hundreds, like ants. Don't compare my disciples to his."

(Sri Sarada Devi, the Great Wonder)

Wisdom Facets From the Gem of Truth

Painting by Swami Tadatmananda

Swami Vivekananda   Sister Nivedita

Nothing does not Exist

"Nothing can be created out of nothing. Everything exists through eternity, and will exist through eternity. This involution and evolution is going on throughout the whole of nature. Only the movement is in succeeding waves and hollows, going back to fine forms, and coming out into gross manifestation. The whole series of evolution beginning with the lowest manifestation of life and reaching up to the higher, the most perfect man, must have been the involution of something else. The question is: The involution of what? What was involved? God."

I Said Virile, not Puerile

"So long as there is desire or want, it is a sure sign that there is imperfection. A perfect, free being cannot have any desire. God cannot want anything. If He desires, He cannot be God. He will be imperfect. So all the talk about God desiring this and that, becoming angry and pleased by turns, is baby's talk, and means nothing. Therefore it has been taught by all true teachers, 'Desire nothing, give up all desires and be perfectly satisfied.'"

Our Father, Not in Heaven

"The heaven envisioned by English people is eternal, and the departed have beautiful bodies and live with their forefathers, and are happy ever after. There they meet with their parents, children, and other relatives and lead very much the same sort of life as here on earth. All the difficulties and obstructions to happiness in this life have vanished, and only its good parts and enjoyments remain. But however comfortable mankind may consider this state of things, Truth is one thing and comfort is another. Truth is not comfortable until we reach its climax. Human nature is very conservative. It does something, and having once done that finds it hard to get out of it. The mind will not receive new thoughts, because they bring discomfort." *(Complete Works of Vivekananda)*

The Motherhood of the Motherland

"A yearning love that can never refuse us; a benediction that forever abides with us; a presence from which we cannot grow away; a heart in which we are always safe; sweetness unfathomed, bond unbreakable, holiness without a shadow — all these and more is indeed Motherhood." *(Eternal Mother)*

India In Her Own Right

"To his [Swami Vivekananda's] mind, Hinduism was not to remain a stationary system, but to prove herself capable of embracing and welcoming the whole modern development. She was no congeries of divided sects, but a single living Mother-Church, recognizing all that had been born of her, fearless of the new, eager for the love of her children, wherever they might be found, wise, merciful, self-directing, pardoning and reconciling. Above all she was the holder of a definite vision, the preacher of a distinct message amongst the nations. To prove her this, however, he relied on no force but that of character." *(Complete Works of Sister Nivedita)*

Dustproof Sacrifice

"Sacrifice is the only means for achieving success in worldly life, but that sacrifice should be completely free from any selfish motive. If, even unconsciously, one's sacrifice is made with a sense of egoism or desire, that valuable effort is ground to dust." *(Nivedita As I Saw Her)*

The Death of Death

"I am thinking, more and more, that Death means just a withdrawal into meditation, the sinking of the stone into the well of its own being. There is the beginning before death, in the long hours of quiescence, when the mind hangs suspended in the characteristic thought of its life, in that thought which is the residuum of all its thoughts and acts and experiences. Already in these hours the soul is disincarnating, and the new life has commenced." *(Sister Nivedita)*

SCRIPTURAL SAYINGS
of the World's Religious Traditions

"For countless lives have I passed through this cycle of births and deaths, seeking the builder of this tabernacle, but in vain. Sorrowful indeed is this cyclic repetition of births and deaths. But now, oh builder of this house, I have seen you; you shall not build the house again. All the rafters are now broken; the ridgepole is sundered. Mind has arrived at dissolution, and through nirvana has attained the extinction of all cravings."

"Blessed am I, blessed, for I have the constant vision of myself. The bliss of Brahman shines clearly to me. I am free of the sufferings of the world. My ignorance has fled away, I know not where. I have no further duty to perform. I have now achieved the highest that one can aspire to. There is nothing that can compare with my great bliss. Blessed am I, blessed, blessed, blessed, again and again blessed!"

"We brought nothing into this world, and it is certain we can carry nothing out. Thus, having food and raiment, let us be content therewith. For they who would be rich fall into many a temptation, and become ensnared by many foolish and hurtful lusts which drown them in destruction and perdition. For love of money is at the root of all evil."

"The way of life lies above to the wise that they may depart from all hells beneath. When the wicked turn away from wickedness and do what is lawful and right, they save their souls alive. That one who considers well and turns away from all transgressions shall surely live. He shall not die."

"When animated by the desire for Allah, a man should not halt for a moment in his quest, nor even shrink from risking his life. The advances he makes correspond directly to the excellence he has been able to acquire, for he can only approach his goal by virtue of his own self-preparation."

"The truly great soul does good but makes little of it, accomplishes great things but gets not attached to them. His secret is that he does not seek to do great things, and that is why he is able to accomplish them. He does not let his wisdom appear, however, and should he succeed in manifesting wondrous deeds and gaining a reputation, he withdraws out of sight before either of these can adhere to him."

UNDYING FEALTY TO JNANAM
The Effects of Self-Knowledge on Spiritual Life

*J*nanam — the destroyer of ignorance, misery, and death — is the very best of all principles, all objectives, all possible attainments available to the people of this earth. It is so, and will always be so. For, in the end, all action, if rightly undertaken, duly leads to knowledge. This why we hear that "Knowledge is father to the deed" – the true and well-thought deed. Tellingly, the luminaries who come to this earth have their own implicit though recondite way of expressing this fact. They embody in the physical realm out of wisdom, not due to ignorance, thereby starting the game, test, trial, play, or sport of life — whatever the human soul calls it or turns it into — on the proper footing.

Most beings, unfortunately, embody in ignorance — both of their birthless, deathless nature, and of the dynamics of the rebirth process itself. It is therefore that a soul's real spiritual evolution begins with the seeking of knowledge, and this also is the beginning of the death of death itself. As my guru used to say, *"We must cause doubt to doubt itself, make fear afraid of itself, and put death in its own grave."* Why is this necessary? Because, as he said on many an occasion, *"From the cradle to the grave, man suffers interminably."* In case the weak and attached mind clinging to relativity wants to find any "wiggle room" in this statement, tradition has it that pleasure is also a type of suffering. Detaching and observing the path of pleasure, called the *Bhoga Marga* by the seers, will reveal this to be true, but this takes an intrepid and spiritually enterprising soul.

The Supreme Justifier

The superlative justification of Wisdom, and the sure and certain measure of its power, effectivity, and supremacy, is that it proves all other qualities, principles, and practices. No doubt that *bhakti* (devotion) and *dhyanam* (meditation) are excellent, but in order to consummate their highest and greatest ends they really require *Karma Yoga*, the Yoga of Selfless Action, to fully mature them and bring them full circle. That is, these two disciplines (*sadhanas*), whether at the stages of practice or mastery, must be tested in the fires of action on earth, in the human body, to bring out their deepest results and thus be rendered undeniably trustworthy.

Yet Karma Yoga, the proving ground for spiritual giants and principles alike, is itself left wholly ineffective and potentially dangerous as a path without the clarifying presence of spiritual Wisdom. As the Lord, Sri Krishna, the God of Love, tells his beloved student in the *Bhagavad Gita*, His Celestial Song, *"Na hi jnanena sadrishyam pavitram iha vidyate — In all the three worlds, oh Arjuna, there is no greater purifier than that of Wisdom. Those who are perfected in Yoga realize this in their own hearts in due time."*

This brings up a mighty fact of existence, one that is often ignored or overlooked by not only the world in general, but by spiritual aspirants treading the path towards enlightenment. The fact is, that all action is insubstantial in the end, undertaken as it is on a playing field (life, mind, and matter) that is ultimately illusory (constantly changing), a willful and desire-based projection of mentally-based materials and phenomena. As Gaudapada has written in his famous *Karika* on the *Mandukya Upanisad*, *"A runner running a race in a dream goes nowhere."*

This analogy means to convey to us that activity in the world affects no real and lasting change, sports no ultimate aim, and realizes no definitive end. At the culmination of our lives, and during the interim as well (in case we have not noticed it due to our confusion and distraction amidst the constant fray of our frenetic activity), no change, aim, or end is achieved. The individual and cosmic cycles merely vibrate onward in interminable fashion, circling systematically, even ominously, with human beings acting like hamsters running on an ever-spinning wheel contained within a cage of self-imposed bondage. As Swami Vivekananda has put it, *"Do not work yourself out. It is of no use. Duty is the midday sun whose fierce rays are burning the very vitals of humanity. It is necessary for a time as a discipline; beyond that it is a morbid dream."*

Waking up from this morbid dream of mental projection to find the ever-stationary Self is to realize that change cannot effect change on an ever-changing ground. Human beings cannot change an always shifting substratum via works. In short, we cannot teach *Maya*, the queen of all transformations, of all legerdemain, any new tricks. The dye has been cast. Now, it is up to the soul to either recognize the pattern and struggle to get free, or be dragged along for lifetimes by *karma's* merciless momentum.

Perceiving the potential bondage of karma-laden activity, then, should human beings cease to work? A better question would be, how can we render work and all activity into helpmates that will free us rather than into chains that bind us? The answer comes, "Through *Jnanam*, how else?" This is where liberating wisdom does the work that other yogas cannot fully accomplish, and it does so most swiftly as well. Mother Wisdom, or discriminating wisdom (*viveka*) as it is called by the seers, is

immediate. The reason why, is that like the freedom it ushers in (*mukti/moksha*), it is sentient, all-pervasive, and eternal — all three. Without it, life and action will invariably waylay the human soul in the cage of worldly life, and then seal it into the coffin of repeated births and deaths in ignorance (*samsara*).

Illumined souls like Lord Buddha noticed the lack of discriminating wisdom in embodied beings, and rued its absence. In the *Dhammapada*, it is written: *"The careless man who exerts stressfully, heedless of higher purpose, scatters karma-laden activities like dust across a plains."* "Karma-laden activities" means work that is engaged in devoid of discriminating wisdom. It not only ruins the present lifetime with its unwanted karmic returns, but also routes the soul into a series of slavish lives based upon *rajas*, restlessness. As Sri Krishna states in the Bhagavad Gita, *"Those who pass from the body in the slothful atmosphere of tamas are reborn in the wombs of the lazy and indeterminate, while those who die with a restless mind are born again to those who are attached to frenetic activity."*

It should also be mentioned here, however, even emphatically, that there are some souls that return to embodiment free of such weights, and able to perceive their inmost Consciousness under any and all situations. Possessing the *viveka* of discriminating wisdom, they pass consciously from one body and return to take up another fully aware of their life's mission — to awaken sleeping souls to their innate perfection.

The chart on the facing page gives an idea of the special powers such souls possess, prior to taking up a fresh body on earth. To them, life is a pure, white canvas upon which they can paint a divine portrait, using the entire spectrum of colors granted to them by spiritual life. This teaching is all the more eye opening when we apply it to the West and its people, whose great industriousness and technical advances are having a mixed effect on human life in these tumultuous times. For such beings as these, and pertaining to both the rajasic and the tamasic soul, Lord Vasishtha states: *"There is no real spiritual progress to be made for those plodding and monotonous beings who occupy the dry plains, infertile valleys, and low-lying marshes of vacuous thought and superficial activity."* To escape this dilemma, what is wanted is *sattva*, balance and equanimity, and that will not come to the human soul without the aspiration for purification that *Jnanam* provides.

The Triple Essence of Jnanam
1) Nitya/Sanatana: Eternal

It has been stated previously that *Jnanam* is eternal. This assertion is not made with reference to time and history alone, but predominantly from the standpoint of locus or locale. Liberating Wisdom is not just a purifier, then; it is a location of the subtlest and most radiant kind. When contemplating it in this way, an aspirant after Truth does not think in terms of physical space alone, as is the tendency of most of today's scientists, physicists, and intellectuals, but must consider a space beyond the ken of atomic particles, consisting of — if the phrase can be allowed — *Atmic* Particles. These consist of pure, sentient, eternally existing Awareness, the kind that insights, visions, and deep realizations are made of. They underlie the *Chid* in *Satchidananda*, a most superlative name for Reality. They represent the *Chid* in *Chidabhasa* as well, the streaming outward of incipient Intelligence before and as it transforms into *lokas*, realms, worlds, objects, as well as the minds and senses of the living beings that behold them.

Pure Intelligence is a flow of sentient particles that is unimpeded by matter, objects, gravity, and other indurate limitations of the physical universe. And just as atomic particles congeal to form the universe of objects in physical space and time, these tiny living bits of pure sentiency coalesce to form a world where knowledge, the act of knowing, and the knower, all abide in perfect harmony, and where those who seek this incomparable blend of nectar-like awareness dwell. Termed *Jnanakasha* by the sages and seers, this luminous land of enlightenment is the locus of emanation of all the realized souls who project themselves into any type of form, and the station of return into which they all merge at the time of leaving physical form.

These illumined souls, like rays from a sun, emit from the realm of Jnana Wisdom upon taking birth, and withdraw their essence from all forms upon their return. The great secret here is that it is the Blessed Lord and Divine Mother alone that are affecting this playful, apparent movement. In the *Bhagavad Gita*, Sri Krishna states: *"An eternal portion of Myself becomes the jiva (embodied soul) in this world, attracting to it the five senses and the mind like flowers attract bees through the redolence in nectar. But none sees Me as I come and go thusly, just as none sees the wind as it takes and delivers scents to and from their various sources."*

In another sloka of the *Gita*, Sri Krishna refers to this unseen process as the "Sunlit Path," as contrasted to the "Moonlit Path" by which a multitude of less aware souls travel inwardly (the Bright and the Dark). The former is the way of those who will soon be performing all action on earth — if they should return there — in the protective atmosphere of liberating knowledge, while the latter is more for those who will only labor interminably in the *"dusty plains of unresolved karma"* without knowing why, wholly bereft of the peace, contentment, and satisfaction that attends upon those who hold *Jnanam*. Both pathways lead to and exist within the "Fields of the Lord," to be sure, but the adherents of these two alternative paths seek according to different methods, i.e., the *Jnana Marga* or the *Bhoga Marga*. The famous declaration in the *Gita* around *Vyavasayatmika*, one-pointed practice, applies nicely here: *"To the firm in mind there is but one decision, but many-branching are the decisions of the infirm in mind."* To seek *Jnanam*, therefore, and apply it to all of life, earthly and spiritual — temporal, terrestrial, and transcendent — is the preoccupation of the "firm in mind."

Within the movement of intelligent particles, the latter soul-way, called the Moonlit Path, is the avenue that is much more populated, coursing between the three worlds of earth, heaven, and subtler heavens (also seen as the three lower *chakras* in the *Kundalini Yoga* system). The transmigration of living beings, due to the constant karmic interchange that goes on with their ancestors, takes place along this sprawling and bustling internal thoroughfare. As Lord Kapila, the Father of *Sankhya Yoga*, declares: *"There are two great streams of consciousness along which billions of transmigrating souls are coursing. One is called Samsara Prag Bhara, and the other, Kaivalya Prag Bhara."*

The Palette of Conscious Future Lives

"Human being — today it is, tomorrow it is not. No one will accompany a person after death. Only actions, good and bad, follow, even after death. The result of karma is inevitable. But karma's effects can be counteracted greatly by japa and austerities." Sri Sarada Devi

Attaining Jivanmukti, Liberation, in a past Lifetime

Selecting the country and culture of one's choice

Assuming gender and physical body

Spiritual practice and attainment in previous Lives

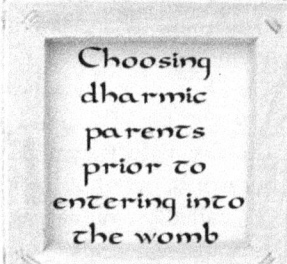
Choosing dharmic parents prior to entering into the womb

Arranging life-circumstances in order to neutralize karma

Experiencing a conscious death at the end of the last Lifetime

"Ego, plus mind, plus intelligence — and adding in the five senses — make up this temporal unit called the psycho-physical being. When considering it and its powers, we must remember that when these eight facets are kept in a pure state, then Kundalini Shakti loves to sport in this amazing form." Lord Vasishtha

Setting up the manifestation of one's work and mission in life

Sincere compassion to help all beings gain spiritual emancipation

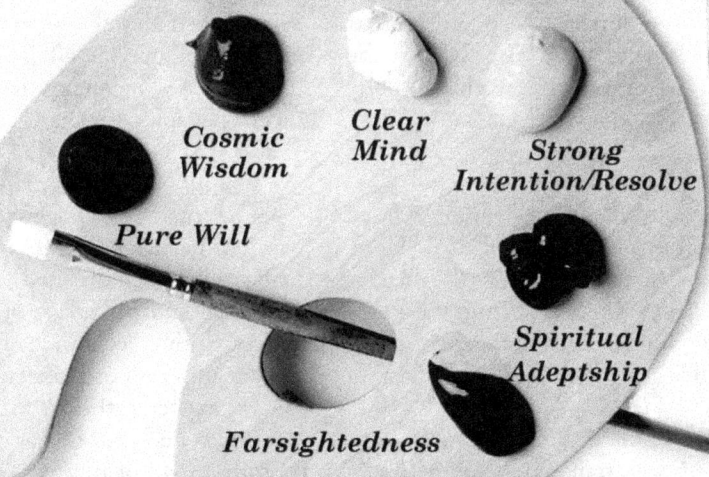
Cosmic Wisdom · Clear Mind · Strong Intention/Resolve · Pure Will · Spiritual Adeptship · Farsightedness

Nondual perspective that transforms all appearances into Reality

"The potter puts his pots in the sun to dry, both the baked and unbaked ones. A cow happens to walk over them and breaks some of them. The baked pot shards that are broken he throws away, but the soft ones, though broken, he gathers up and shapes them into a lump. From this lump he forms new pots. In the same way, so long as a man has not realized God, he will have to come back to this earth — to the Potter's Hands." Sri Ramakrishna Paramahamsa

Chart by Babaji Bob Kindler   Property of SRV Associates

> "These *Samanvaya Mahacharyas* hail from the *Jnanakasha*, the realms of living Intelligence. They do not speciate from Nature; they radiate from living Awareness. For the most part they are not recognized by their human counterparts, whose flowing Intelligence has not awakened yet."

The words, "prag bhara," refer to a dam that restricts an otherwise unimpeded flow. Like a clog-up on an interstate highway, called a "traffic jam," similarly, the inner avenues of samsara are conducting a multitude of souls, like cars or vehicles (*upadhis*), to destinations unsatisfactory and unsavory, and with many long, aggravating stops along the way. These coarse thoroughfares are coming from, leading to, and ending up in *samsara,* all based upon the stunted state of mind of hosts of souls steeped in collective ignorance of their formless, all-intelligent nature. To leave this crazy network of accident-prone internal highways is *to steer one's soul-vehicle towards Kaivalya, or Freedom. In this quest, Jnanam* is true Freedom's adept and versatile assistant.

To decrease the state of incredulity around things spiritual, and to help explain the flow of subtle energy and intelligent particles, we must imagine a huge road map that contains all freeways, avenues, roads, streets, and even back alleyways. Now we are to envision that this map reveals the layout of the inner worlds rather than of physical continents alone. In other words, its network of roads consists of unseen, undetected nerves, called *nadis,* all conducting the dream-energy of transmigrating souls.

Along this subtle network of nerve pathways is moving an infinite plethora of souls, unseen by physical eyes in the realm of atomic particles; this is how beings both enter and depart the body, as well as the earth plane. So, this vision also demonstrates where beings go after death and before rebirth. The difference between these two realms is that the subtle one shows the movement of a living force of intelligent particles, rather than an insentient force consisting of material particles. Awareness of this distinction empowers the soul to take charge of its future choices (see chart on pg 27) and destinations, up and until it merges consciously in its own pristine Nature. The chart on the facing page (pg 29) conveys an idea of the inner worlds of subtle nadis, or the "....many chambers of My Father's Mansion."

2) Ajada/Buddhi-purva: Living, Sentient

Jnanam's second essential quality, mentioned earlier, is fused intrinsically to the existence of it as a living intelligence. Here, when we inquire of the tradition, we find that just as the mind is different from the brain, intelligence is different from the intellect. The latter is a sheath, a container, even a covering, while the former is, as described above, an essentially-aware flow of sentient wisdom particles.

The word "sentiency" is one of the best in the English language to describe the difference between mankind and nature, a distinction that naturally assists the soul in the process that the Indian seers call *viveka,* and the Buddhists call *khyati* — a wise, spiritually-based discernment that adroitly allocates Spirit and Matter, God and Mammon, to their respective places. Peace of mind follows this crucial categorization....for the few who would move to attain and apply it.

Following what is intrinsically alive, then, the aspiring soul so tempers and refines his or her awareness so as to be able to enter, at will, the flow of intelligent particles, thus the realm of real Wisdom, not just secular knowledge. This leads to what the luminaries covet the most, namely, direct perception of Reality — *Pratyaksham*. Looking outward towards the dreamlike worlds of becoming, or gazing within towards the more sublime climes of radiant Awareness, the enlightened soul can do both. This makes him/her proficient as both a sterling example and an adept teacher, depending on which trajectory is selected. Since these great souls know the world's two eternal paths — the Bright and the Dark, the Sunlit and the Moonlit — the final decision is always up to them. Living, flowing Intelligence forms a stream of consciousness by which they pass to and from, or in and out of the many worlds of embodying souls.

And since they are in possession of sentient intelligence, they appear on earth in the most peaceful and blissful of bodies and (mental) conditions, and act as the best unifiers of all human aspirations. These *Samanvaya Mahacharyas* hail from the *Jnanakasha,* the realms of living Intelligence. They do not speciate from Nature; they radiate from living Awareness. For the most part they are not recognized by their human counterparts, whose flowing Intelligence has not awakened yet. Therefore, these beings of absolute Sentiency must act as prime examples for the attainment of what is highest and best in the world. Their cherished aim is a type of intelligence that is extraordinary, even in the realm of *Jnanam. It is* called *Alaya-vijnana,* wisdom accompanied by the ideal of Universality. To spread this most sublime of ideals is at the back of every thought and act that they undertake for the benefit of humanity, for they have realized its supreme efficacy due to their rapt exploration of the many *lokas* lying along this ever-flowing wisdom stream of intelligent particles.

3) Vyapti/Sarvagatah: All-Pervasiveness

To comprehend deeply the ramifications of these streams of wisdom particles that inundate the mind at all levels (cosmic, collective, and individual), it is most helpful to internally imbibe the ideal and personage of the Wisdom Mother Herself. Only then can one get an idea of how swift is Her Intelligence, and how it infills all of Existence.

Existence is the *Sat* in *Satchidananda,* Its Pure Being. Just as sweetness permeates sugar cane juice, so too does *Jnanam* literally saturate all of Existence. In its mode or aspect of all-pervasiveness, Her eternal, living Intelligence is unimaginably swift. Faster than the speed of sound is the speed of light; faster than the speed of light is the speed of thought. But faster than thought is this immediate presence of Intelligence out of which exceptionally keen thoughts arise. That startling and all-encompassing imminence is due to its quality of all-pervasiveness.

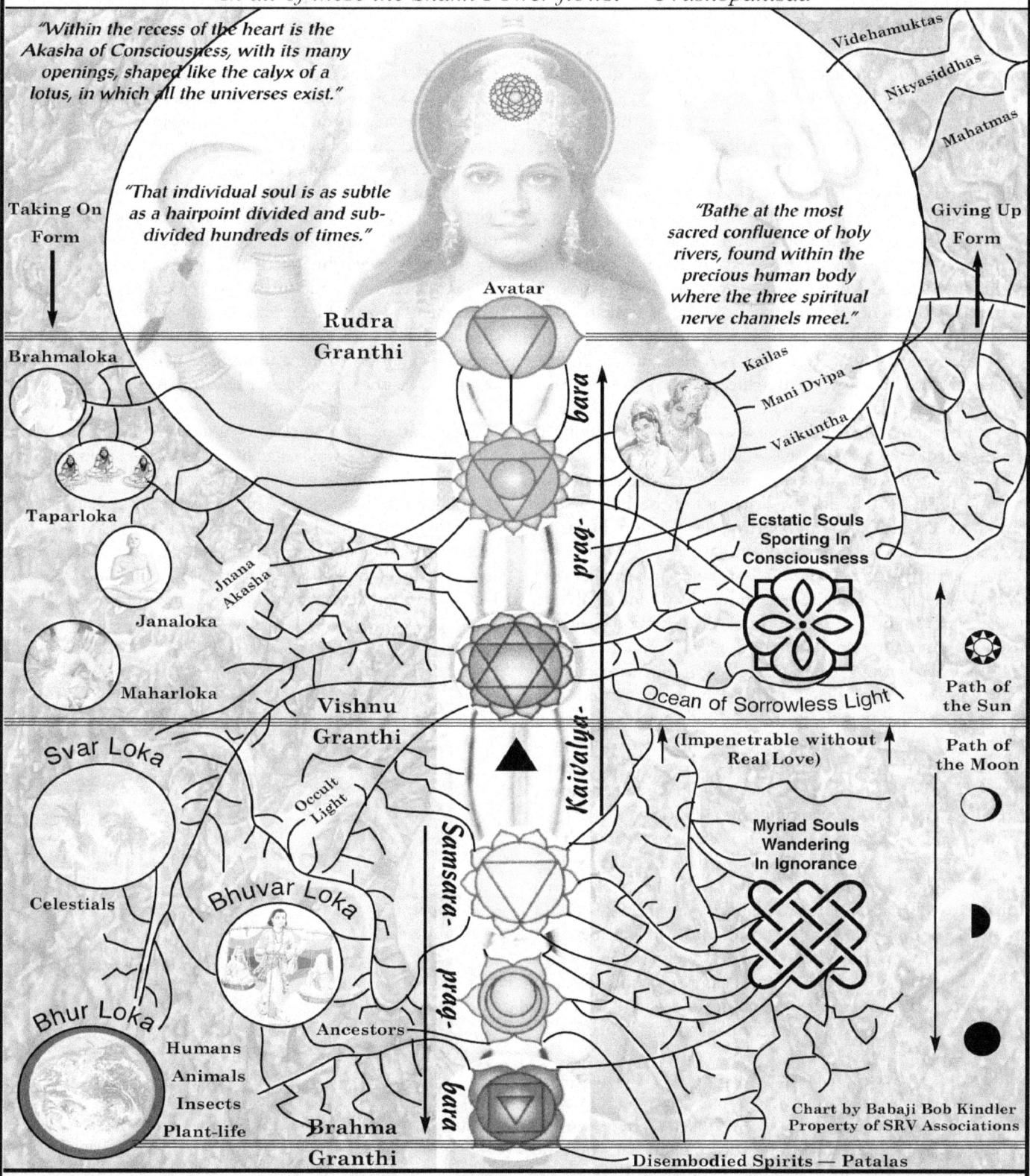

That is why it is called *avicchinna*, undivided, and *atindriya*, beyond any knowledge that is available to the mind and senses. As the *Ishavasyopanisad* states, "*It is One. It is faster than the mind. It is beyond the reach of the senses. Ever steady, yet it outstrips all that run. By its mere presence it enables the cosmic energy to sustain the activities of living beings.*"

Along with the inherently living nature of Intelligence, the all-pervasiveness of Intelligence has another secret to unfold. That is, and as the Holy Mother, Sri Sarada Devi, has said, "*Objects are just thought made manifest.*" When the ordinary mind, being accustomed to conventional scientific thinking about the nature of matter, inspects the same, it sees what it expects, and does so on the level it is presently operating. But when the mind of a luminary, aware of the presence of everything as Consciousness manifesting in form, scrutinizes nature, matter, and objects, it sees the congealing of the projecting power of Intelligence. Everything — objects, nature, possessions, food — is perceived as wisdom in form, as thought concretized. Thus, the worldly see all as matter meant for possessions and pleasures, but the seer perceives all as living Intelligence. And here is where true life, with its all-encompassing, all-containing bliss, proceeds from. Therefore, those in possession of discriminating Wisdom view true life and real living as eternal, sentient, and all-pervasive — all three.

To help the Western mind, accustomed to the scientific way of viewing things, to fathom the teachings of the Indian seers (*rishis*) on the crucial role of Intelligence, the chart on the facing page (page 31) takes up the now familiar subject of particles, revealing, as the *Upanisads* often refer to, what is "*minuter than an atom.*" The gist is that the human mind will not be able to find what is most subtle, transcendent of relativity, and ultimately real, by examining increments of physical matter alone. Though it is fascinating to see that physical objects consist of many various kinds of particles, it will be much more interesting and engaging to discover the truth that both objects and their particles exist within one's own consciousness — as pure Intelligence. As the Zen teaching relates, in order to behold the mystery of one's Consciousness, the seer will have to examine it as carefully as an Eskimo examines snow conditions.

This secret, as far as the nature of particles is concerned, consists of performing this examination inwardly, like in deep meditation. For this experiment to be successful, both the belief that matter is all that exists, as well as the outward trajectory of brain and senses, will have to be abandoned. Just as measurement based on the micron scale, giving way later to a finer gauge called nanometers, was helpful to the scientist at one point, so too will more definitive aid come when the understanding dawns that there are particles that transcend the physical plane and escape matter entirely.

Following the right hand side of the chart (facing page) upwards, this transition of particles from gross, to subtle, to causal, and beyond, can be traced. *Anna matra*, the name the ancient rishis had for tiny material particles, disappear when the mind's awareness perceives the subtle worlds within, or enters the dream state. Particles of life-force, called *prana*, form the next plateau of consciousness, and subtle bodies — like those of the departed ancestors and celestials — abide there.

Siddhanta: An Apt Conclusion

And here we return to activity and work. Since spirituality is such a rare thing in the everyday experience of modern man, and higher intelligence such an unseen, unknown facet of mankind's consciousness, the cultivation of the awareness of *Jnanam* at a more rudimentary level will be practical and best. As Sri Ramakrishna has remarked, "*The superior swordsman fences with two blades.*" That is to say, activity alone is insufficient to the task it seeks to accomplish. Only when the second blade, *Jnanam*, swift and sharp, is brought into the picture can work be trusted to affect and sustain any real progress in life.

Otherwise, no real or abiding intelligence visits our activities, either now (present lifetime) or later (future lives), which is why a work-a-day world is both undesirable and dangerous as an ultimate goal. As Swami Vivekananda has explained, what we want is work as worship, labor as love, and service as selflessness.

And as we wend our way towards comprehending and implementing this higher vision and goal, the presence and application of *Jnanam* will turn out to be the wisest and most effective addition to life and mind that the struggling soul can resort to. As the Great Master has explained, "*Intelligence, devotion, compassion, and renunciation — such qualities as these belong to the realm of true Knowledge. With these a man comes near to God. One more step and he attains God! But a man's intelligence is very delicate, and can get covered, distorted, or misled. He must therefore practice austerities so as to acquire Divine Knowledge.*"

May this Divine Knowledge attend upon us in its entirety, and with immediate celerity, so that Peace, *Shanti*, may come unto all, the highest good may betide all, and that all may see the face of Truth, and be fortified by the armor of Love.

Babaji Bob Kindler is the Spiritual Director of the SRV Associations with centers in Hawaii, Oregon, and California. A teacher of religion and spirituality and a prolific author, his books include *The Avadhut, Twenty-Four Aspects of Mother Kali, Ten Divine Articles of Sri Durga, Sri Sarada Vijnanagita, Swami Vivekananda Vijnanagita, An Extensive Anthology of Sri Ramakrishna's Stories, A Quintessential Yoga Vasishtha, Reclaiming Kundalini Yoga, and others.* Founder and Artistic Director of Jai Ma Music, he is also an accomplished musician and composer who has produced over twenty-five albums of instrumental and devotional music to date.

From Atomic Particles to "Atmic" Particles

"Verily, that one indivisible Consciousness is the indwelling Essence in all things. Fire is Its head, the sun and moon, Its two eyes, and the unstruck sound, Om, Its ears. The revelation of scripture is Its cosmic mind, the many-tiered universe of name and form, from gross to subtle, Its heart, and Its arms and legs, the four directions. Truth is Its voice, the wind is Its breath, and from Its feet the verdant earth has originated."

Mundakopanisad

Absolute Reality
Absence of all particles, all form

↓

Causal Body
Particles of formless intelligence held in abeyance and potential

↓

Subtle Body
Particles of conceptual thought projected as multiple expressions

↓

Astral Body
Particles of desire-based thought caught in dream states and fantasizing

↓

Physical Body
Particles of dense mental vibration congealed into objects

↓

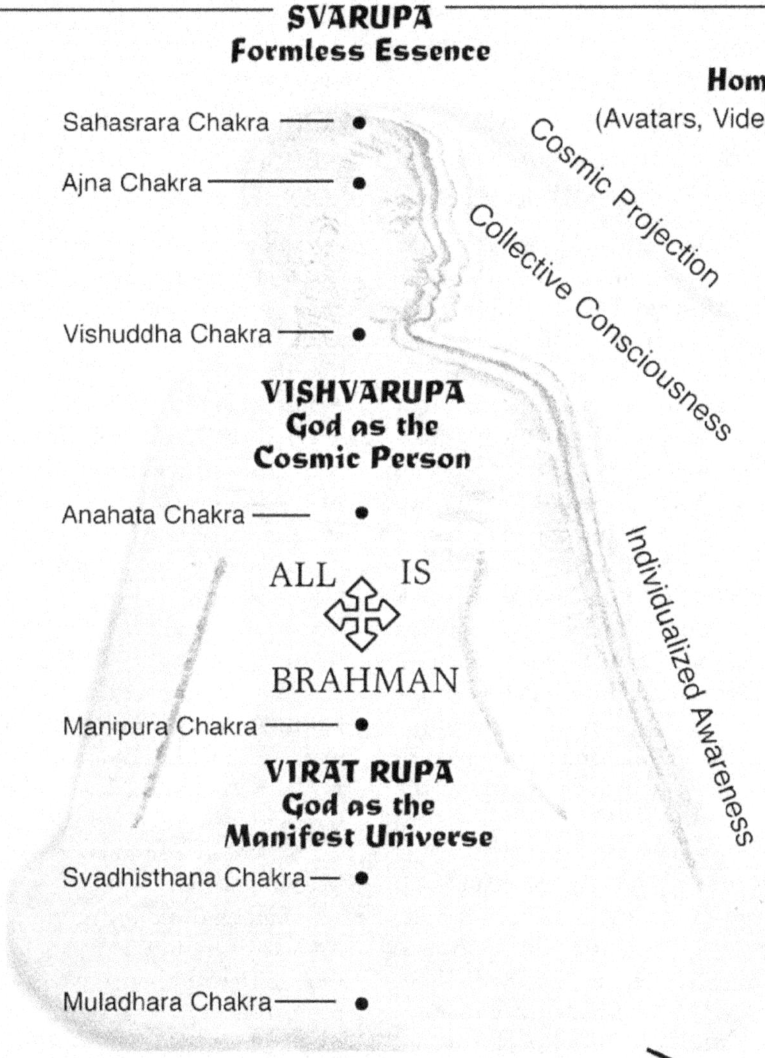
SVARUPA
Formless Essence
Sahasrara Chakra
Ajna Chakra
Vishuddha Chakra
VISHVARUPA
God as the
Cosmic Person
Anahata Chakra
ALL IS BRAHMAN
Manipura Chakra
VIRAT RUPA
God as the
Manifest Universe
Svadhisthana Chakra
Muladhara Chakra
Cosmic Projection
Collective Consciousness
Individualized Awareness

BRAHMAN
Homogenous Awareness
(Avatars, Videhamuktas, Nityasiddhas)
(Turiya)

LAYA MATRA, AUM
Dissolution of all Particles
(The Trinity — Brahma, Vishnu, Siva)
(Deep Sleep)

JNANA MATRA
Particles of Intelligence
(Seers, sages, rishis, yogis)

CHIT MATRA
Particles of Thought
(Gods/Goddesses, munis, siddhas)

PRANA MATRA
Particles of Life-force
(Celestials, ancestors, elementals)
(Dream State)

ANNA MATRA
Particles of Matter
(Humans, animals, insects, plants)
(Waking State)

Disappearance of physical space

Hydrogen atom — 1/10th of a nanometer (nm)
A glucose particle — 1 nanometer
A DNA molecule — 2.5 nanometers
Quantum Physics — Deals in lengths that are less than 10 nm

Classic Physics — Deals in lengths that are greater than 100 nm
Red blood cell — 5000 nm (1 nm = 1 billionth of a meter)
Smallest particle viewable by the naked eye — 1 micron (μm)
A human hair — 50 microns

"Like a lump of sugar dissolving into a cup of tea, the entire world of name and form, and all objects, merge into Brahman, the Ultimate Reality, at the end of a cosmic cycle. All manifested things are soluble into the supremely unmanifested Brahman." *Sri Ramakrishna Paramahamsa*

Chart by Babaji Bob Kindler

Property of SRV Associations

◆ SUZANNE SCHIER-HAPPELL

"I have a Mother"

Sri Sarada Devi, Womanhood, and Modern American Culture

With the many modes of communication we have available to us today, it is lamentable that a greater solidarity among the various families of Vedanta is not more prevalent — as SRV's founder, Lex Hixon, worked so hard for in his life. Thus, we are grateful to print an article of this type, since it points to this missing element, and also allows the hidden voices of so many of our spiritual brethren to be heard.

Over a century ago, Swami Vivekananda planted the seeds of Vedanta in America with the hope that they would someday take root and blossom into a beautiful movement of religious unity and universal truth on American soil. As a result, today a deeply spiritual Vedanta tradition has indeed taken root throughout North America, with practitioners representing a diverse range of ages, genders, cultures, ethnicities, and religious backgrounds. While Vedantins in America espouse a wide variety of beliefs and walk diverse yogic paths, one principle which unites many Vedanta practitioners who follow in Vivekananda's footsteps is devotion to Sri Ramakrishna Paramahamsa and Sri Sarada Devi.

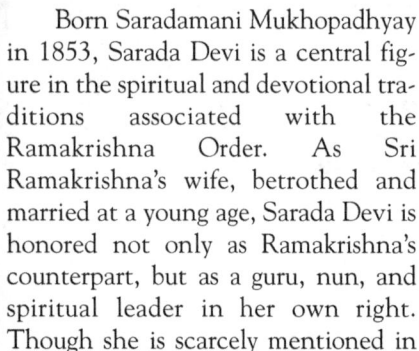

Born Saradamani Mukhopadhyay in 1853, Sarada Devi is a central figure in the spiritual and devotional traditions associated with the Ramakrishna Order. As Sri Ramakrishna's wife, betrothed and married at a young age, Sarada Devi is honored not only as Ramakrishna's counterpart, but as a guru, nun, and spiritual leader in her own right. Though she is scarcely mentioned in the Gospel of Sri Ramakrishna, it being a male disciple's record of conversations that occurred in the gender-segregated gatherings of the 19th century, Sarada Devi became the trustee of Sri Ramakrishna's spiritual teachings, attracting disciples of her own after Sri Ramakrishna's passing. As his widow, Sarada Devi played a critical role in shaping the ongoing spiritual movement begun by Ramakrishna. Today, Sri Sarada Devi occupies a prominent place in the devotional life of practitioners within the Ramakrishna-based Vedanta tradition — both in North America and around the world.

Surveying Spiritual Ground

In order to get a clearer vision of the breadth of spiritual experience related to Sarada Devi, especially in North America, I surveyed Vedanta practitioners about their personal understandings and experiences of her and her teachings. I used an anonymous online survey, distributed voluntarily by contacts at Vedanta Societies and Centers throughout the United States and Canada. One hundred forty-nine people responded to this survey, and among the respondents who provided demographic information:
• 50% were female; 50% were male.
• 1.4% were under 18; 2.2% were 20-29 years; 19.9% were 30-39 years; 17.6% were 40-49 years; 12.5% were 50-59 years; 25% were 60-69 years; 16.2% were 70-79 years; and 5.1% were 80-89 years.
• 50.6% were of Indian/South Asian descent; 40.4% were Caucasian; 2.7% were Latino/-a; 2.7% self-identified as having Jewish ancestry; 2.7% identified as Asian without further distinction; and 0.6% were Native American.

While the overwhelming majority of responses were from North America, I also received responses from throughout the world. Of those who noted their location:
• 70.2% were in the United States; 12.8% were in India; 10.1% were in Canada; 2% were in Latin America; 2% were in Africa; 1.3% were in Southeast Asia; 0.7% were in Europe; and 0.7% were in Australia.

Among those within the United States:
• 41.3% were in the West; 32.6% were in the Northeast; 9.6% were in the Southwest; 8.6% were in the Midwest; 2.9% were in the Southeast; 1% were in Hawaii; and 3.8% did not note their specific location.

I also asked those surveyed whether they grew up in the practice of Ramakrishna traditions, or whether they became devotees later in their lives:
• 71.1% became devotees later in life; 22.8% grew up in the tradition; 2.7% reported both growing up in the tradition and becoming devotees later in life; and 3.3% did not specify.

Unsurprisingly, most people who report growing up in the tradition are of Indian descent; likewise, most Vedantins who are not of Indian descent report becoming devotees later in life. Among this group, a first encounter with the Ramakrishna tradition came either through books (usually either The Gospel of Ramakrishna or the writings of Swami Vivekananda), through people close to them who were already initiated devotees, or through visiting a Vedanta Society for the first time and feeling a sense of connection with the place and people there.

Foundational Experiences of Sarada Devi

As devotees reflected upon their spiritual connections to Sarada Devi, there were several themes shared across all demographic cross-sections of those surveyed. The feeling most frequently, and most passionately, reported is a sense of unconditional love and acceptance, often framed in terms of maternal love:

"The Mother of us all. Non-judgmental and loving of all persons. The real thing. Makes me feel loved and valued highly, and supported always."

"I feel completely accepted and embraced."

"Love incarnate. Makes me feel protected by the divinity and surrounded by love."

"Her love and compassion for an insignificant person like me is something beyond words, expression, or thoughts."

"This is the age of the Holy Mother! SHE is needed everywhere and is removing Her veil so that all may know: I have a Mother! SHE embodies compassion and love and harmony and unconditional acceptance. SHE is the axis mundi of my life and the one to whom I turn for all support and guidance."

There is also a sense that love is not only received by Sarada Devi, but is also actively cultivated in the devotee as a response:

"We are a part of each other. When thinking of Her, I am overwhelmed with love for others."

"When I meditate on her, as I was instructed, I feel a presence of compassion and connection with everything about me."

Another common theme is a sense of strength and empowerment:

"I feel assured and strong when I think of her, and all kinds of fears are allayed."

"Gives me the necessary courage to overcome weaknesses in my character."

"When I think of her I feel some power within me to overcome all obstacles."

Devotees also reported feeling that they are never alone, frequently repeating the affirmation, "I have a Mother!" to describe her abiding presence in their lives:

"She makes me feel like I have a real, eternal Mother, who is constantly with me."

"She makes me feel cared for, and comforted. Like I have a mother."

"She is my real mother, always available when I choose to connect with her. She embodies peace, love, and divinity."

"My own Mother. When I feel that she is my own Mother, I get confidence, peace, and strength. She makes me feel that she and thus God is my own."

Sarada Devi's affirmation that all of her devotees indeed "have a real Mother" becomes especially meaningful to those who have lost their mothers in bodily form, or who have a difficult relationship with their biological mothers:

"Not long after attending the Providence Vedanta Center, my mother suddenly passed away at 51 years old. Holy Mother embraced me with her Eternal Love from that moment and has walked and guided me in my life every day since. Yes, I truly do HAVE A MOTHER!"

"So many women like myself lack a close bond with a biological mother. Mother is that presence personified for me."

Similarly, the following experiences were recounted by men who had lost their wives and were faced with the task of raising children without mothers physically present:

"I was a widowed graduate student with two children. I focused on her and asked her for a mother (human) for my children. My prayer was answered."

"My daughter was not quite six when her mother died, so she really needed a mama. I told her that we all had another mother and that she would always be with us. She became very attached to Holy Mother and the Virgin of Guadalupe."

Sarada Devi's maternal role also allows practitioners to graciously receive guidance from her, sometimes experienced in terms of parental discipline:

"She is my teacher, who rules my mind and when I make a mistake she gently reminds me what I did was wrong. She makes me feel secured and loved; I feel she cares for me all the time regardless of what I do."

In some cases, devotees had a difficult time articulating their connection to Sarada Devi using conventional language, and instead described the emotional response she creates in them:

"I can't put how she makes me feel into words, how I feel is beyond words, but there are times I feel like bursting into tears when looking at her picture. I know in my heart she is a special and a holy woman."

"Thinking about her gets me in touch with my True Self and that leads to a feeling of freedom that cannot be described in words."

"Mama, my all, I grab her by the sari and hold on. I ask and ask and ask, and She answers, through everything. I need to pay attention so I don't miss those responses. Such emotion fills my chest that I cry."

Overall, the universal love, acceptance, and strength of Sarada Devi specifically in her motherly role were themes that

arose in the overwhelming majority of responses, regardless of location, gender, or ethnic background.

Relating to Women

One question I asked practitioners was whether they believed women relate to Sarada Devi in a special way. There were a wide range of responses. Some devotees believe that the universal nature of her message to the world transcends physical distinctions, including gender:

"No, to her all are equal."

"She is first and foremost a mother who knows no gender."

"Both women and men can relate to Holy Mother in the exact same way. When we move the mind past gender, there is no need to relate to Holy Mother as a woman but as a Divine being."

"Probably yes since she was a woman; however, I think of her as transcending sex. In this regard I believe on a higher level she relates no less to men than to women."

"Holy Mother's love and affection was directed towards the whole of creation and the supreme reality. In this way, she has shown the road to supreme love and peace, regardless of one's gender."

In fact, not only do some devotees believe gender is irrelevant and should be disregarded, but some actually went so far as to suggest that focusing on Sarada Devi specifically as a woman (or by any other external distinction) may be spiritually problematic:

"I personally do not emphasize her gender. She is beyond any gender. So are we. Both men and women can benefit from her life and teachings by staying focused on her core message. In fact, I believe, giving too much emphasis on her as a woman can mislead us away from the goal of life."

"Her message is that she is everyone's mother, so she is equally relevant to anyone who is willing to surrender to her holy feet. This is the Oneness Vedanta preaches. How old you are, what color you are, what country you live in, etc., has absolutely no relevance. What matters is this: do you have undying devotion, and are you fully surrendered? If you are not holding anything back for sure that relationship will be relevant ALL the time, and you won't be able to live without it!!!!"

Another perspective supporting the view that gender makes no difference rests on the assertion that all relationships with her are unique; therefore, generalizing about any collective experience of her (for example, the experience of women in general) is impossible, and should instead be approached on an individual basis:

"I think everyone has a unique relationship with Mother. Gender is irrelevant."

"Her life and teachings are meant for all genders and all age groups. Everyone develops a special relationship with her when they read her life or meditate on her."

"I think men and women relate equally to her. We all need her!"

On the other hand, some practitioners did report feeling a special connection to Sarada Devi specifically as a woman. Women especially seemed to find her to be a powerful example, precisely because they could see themselves in her. Consider these two women's responses:

"Yes, women relate to Holy Mother in a special way because within all women, there is this wonderful Mother Sarada Devi. All women are manifestations of Divine Mother, and I think they feel this inner connection with her."

"Yes, because she is an incarnation of God as a woman. We can be just like her. My guru used to tell me this."

In fact, some devotees reported feeling particularly empowered as women by Sarada Devi's example, and saw her as an example of quiet yet unwavering strength:

"Mother, a rising of the feminist strength."

"She inspires a confidence in me that being a woman and a mother I can transcend all barriers and reach the ultimate truth."

"Mother shows women the divinity within themselves. She reminds

women of their strength and power."

Some women specifically addressed the way they felt Sarada Devi challenged patriarchal social and religious norms as well:

"She was the body proof of Vivekananda's conviction, five women could accomplish what only 100 men could. She had been the source of inspiration to face it all in sheer endurance… She never compromised with unholiness."

"I was raised in a [religious] tradition with a very masculine image of God, where God was always portrayed as angry and judgmental. Holy Mother's loving embrace was such a relief compared to the religious fear I was raised with, and her divinity affirms that not only are women not inferior to men, but women have equal spiritual potential and are just as connected to God as men. She makes me feel worthy."

Some women also expressed a feeling of connection with Sarada Devi through a shared experience of obstacles unique to women in society:

"I would think so [that women relate to her in a special way] because she had to face so much of the prejudice women do as to limitations on their spirituality, career, etc."

In contrast to the opinions expressed above, still another perspective emerged, challenging the legitimacy of the question completely! These respondents questioned whether it is even possible to relate to Sarada Devi at all because of the loftiness of her divinity:

"Relating to Holy Mother in any way is very difficult. She had no trace of lower Nature present in her. She was functioning at the heart level and above."

While there were a wide variety of responses to this question, a majority of women surveyed did indeed believe that women could relate to Sarada Devi in a special way.

Equality, Selflessness, and Rejecting Judgment of Others

I also asked for opinions about the relevance of Sarada Devi to modern life in North America. There were several common themes which emerged among these replies, with one being her emphasis on equality and inclusion among all people:

"When the world is divided on race, religion, nationality, color, it is very important to remember Mother saying, 'Nobody is a stranger, my child. Know that the whole world is your own.' This is universal love and is very relevant today."

"Her message of inclusion is greatly needed in the world today. Treating and loving everyone equally is what we need to heal our hearts and minds."

"The ease with which she interacted with women from different cultures and overlooked differences also provides a very sound example for us in the US."

"Her message of universal love and acceptance is especially important in this age of intolerance."

Several respondents specifically focused upon a fear of "the other" which they perceived to be growing in American society. They believed Sarada Devi's teachings to be capable of countering this negativity with selflessness and universal acceptance:

"There is too much prejudice, fear, and strife being promoted against 'the other' by… politicians. As brothers and sisters, we need to practice the golden rule more in our everyday lives."

"We live in an era of amazing xenophobia and judgmentalism… I believe the Holy Mother's teachings are exactly what we need to move us toward being a kinder, more benevolent, and more spiritual civilization. I notice that people always try to find fault with others first. Nothing is ever their fault. It's always someone else… The Holy Mother's teaching will reverse this egotism."

"When there is so much unrest and selfishness in the fast-paced world, where everyone thinks, 'What is there in it for me?' Sri Sarada Devi's message comes ringing… 'How can I serve you?'"

Modesty, Restraint, and Body Image

There were also a number of responses exploring the value of modesty and restraint in a culture which often celebrates the opposite, especially for women. The following responses all come from women reflecting upon this topic:

"Her teachings are very relevant in America. There is no role model like this for us here. She provides a powerful example of chastity which is so important and underrated here."

"Her modesty is an example to young women today who are bombarded by sexual and anorexic images in the media that cause low self-esteem."

"I think women are so often defined by our physical appearance and sexuality in today's American culture. There is so much pressure to have the perfect body, the perfect face, the perfect clothes. Body shaming is a constant. There are eating disorders and self-esteem problems resulting from insecurity about how we look, and there is a constant preoccupation with sex all around us. But I do not want to be defined by my body, nor do I want to be reduced to my sexuality. These things objectify women. They make me feel objectified. Here also, Mother

shows us another way. Her example of modesty, restraint, and transcendence of sexuality represent to me a rejection of these harmful, misogynistic values which objectify women… To me, claiming my sexual freedom means choosing restraint… No one is entitled to my body but me… I suppose some people who don't understand might look at this as repressive, but to me, it is liberating."

Sarada Devi appears to provide a powerful counter-narrative to a view of femininity focused on physical appearances and sexuality. Interestingly, though, this more restrained view of womanhood is still often framed in terms of freedom, autonomy, and self-esteem (versus duty or submission).

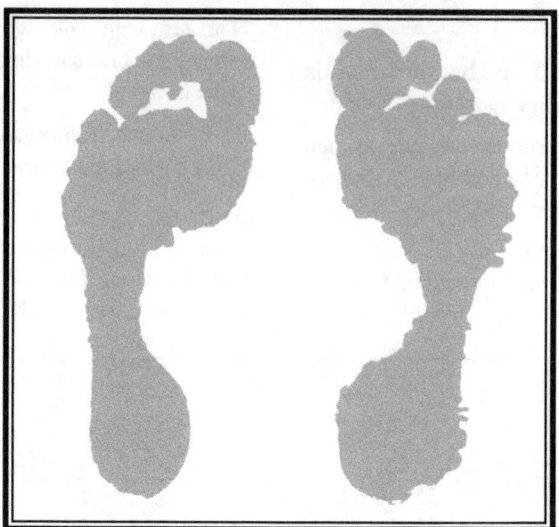

Spiritual Focus in a Materialistic World

Many practitioners also noted the overwhelming materialism of American culture, and identified Sarada Devi's example as a means to overcome this materialism. Some of the important examples of this are as follows:

"We are so materialistic; people place so much importance on building wealth to define their success, and on having certain possessions to define their identities. Mother rejected both of these ideas and instead focused on the eternal. It is not things that define us, but rather it is our behaviors, our love for others, our devotion to God, our sincerity… I think materialism is responsible for a lot of the suffering people experience today in our culture. Mother shows us another way."

"In America, there is too much emphasis on materialism and petty grievances… If people opened themselves to the underlying spiritual realities, they would be much happier and healthier… Seeking answers for one's misery in oneself rather than looking outward for someone to blame is one of the messages I have received from Sri Sarada Devi."

This theme of rejecting the outwardness of materialism and instead turning inward to focus on spiritual ideals continued to emerge:

"I think we Americans desperately need her teachings. We have become staunch materialists. We fight among ourselves over the smallest slight. We are greedy and selfish. Mother teaches a way of loving and giving indiscriminately, which helps us grow in compassion, wisdom, and joy."

"When life is turning towards materialism more and more, and 'keeping up with the Joneses' seems to be the motto of the day, Holy Mother's teachings remind you to take a step back and reevaluate one's needs vs. wants in the perspective of the goal of our life. It reminds us to do our duty in full-earnest and leave the rest to the Lord."

"She is going to be the solace of a nation like America once the materialistic tendencies disgust people and they realize that peace cannot be obtained that way. The more this realization will rise, which already started I see, the more Americans and Westerners will discover her depth and divinity."

Ultimately, a number of respondents expressed an expectation that attempts to find joy through physical wealth would ultimately fail, leading more people to pursue true happiness through spiritual rather than material means — happiness which could be attainable by following the perfectly natural example of the Holy Mother, Sri Sarada Devi.

Conclusion

The responses detailed here represent only a small sampling of many incredible stories and experiences shared by devotees about their connections to Sri Sarada Devi. It has been an honor and a privilege to be entrusted with these reflections, and what amazes me the most as I look over these responses is how many ways there are to approach and experience Mother — how her teachings and example continue to find relevance transcending the physical distinctions of location, gender, culture, or any other physical quality.

While Sarada Devi's ultimate significance may indeed be beyond our limited understanding, all devotees strive to connect with her in their own special manner. By seeing how a variety of people describe her impact on their lives through so many unique perspectives, may we all be inspired to experience Holy Mother in new and meaningful ways.

Suzanne Schier-Happell is a full-time Instructor in the Religion and Philosophy Department at Otterbein University in Westerville, Ohio, teaching classes on Hinduism, Buddhism, and religion/gender. Suzanne received her M.A. in History and Critical Theories of Religion from Vanderbilt University in 2001, and her B.A. in Religion and Culture from Emory University in 1998. She also completed additional graduate work in Sanskrit and South Asian religions at the University of Wisconsin-Madison. Currently, she is writing a doctoral dissertation—of which the research presented here is a small part—for Hindu University of America under the supervision of her most respected teacher, Swami Tyagananda. To learn more about her research, to participate in her survey—or simply to make a meaningful connection—you are warmly invited to write to her at shappell@otterbein.edu.

The Law of Consequences
The Inscrutable Law of Karma

In today's scientific age we have become aware, to some extent, of the laws that govern the physical world of Nature. But to accept that human nature is controlled by subtle laws just as physical nature is governed by physical laws, is very difficult. The ancient Indian rishis asserted that human energy, in its manifested form as thought, emotion, or action, also follows subtle laws of cause and effect. We are unable to understand even physical laws, bereft of the mathematical framework. Psychological laws are even more difficult to understand because there is no other means for the mind to measure itself! Take for instance the law of consequences. This is the basic idea in the *Bhagavad Gita* — that whatever we do, think, feel, will have a consequence. That is, the law of consequence is fundamental to us. We believe that we are free to do whatever we like, think, feel, and say, and there will be no consequence! Vedic psychology says there is a consequence to every action, spoken word, thought, or feeling. In this age it is very difficult to acknowledge that we suffer the consequences of our own making. Our past is very deep. Therefore we must have the motivation and desire to understand these laws, which were discovered in ancient India and were taken on faith.

Law of Sankalpa

The *Bhagavad Gita* (Chapter VI, slokas 2 & 4) points to *sankalpa* as a subconscious motive, which means that before we start any activity we have already, somewhat, made a mental note of the result we want or expect from that activity. It sounds normal and natural that we have already decided what we want as the outcome of a particular activity, emotion or thought; not to look for results seems abnormal. To work for the sake of work is for extraordinary people, or so we think. We do not take the law of consequence seriously! The word *sankalpa* in Sanskrit is used in a very technical way. We focus on what we expect or want, and automatically our anticipation does not see the outcome as a consequence, which will not necessarily be as per our expectation! The *Bhagavad Gita* points out that *sankalpa* is always there. Therefore, we need to be aware and be prepared. The real causes for the transformation of our mental energy are within. If we really want the truth, we will face all the consequences and learn thereby.

For example, we believe that the earth on which we live is steady, when it is not. Think of the volatility of an earthquake. If we were conscious of the movement of the globe, or of the tectonic plates, etc., we would know of the inevitability of earthquakes and tsunamis, and would therefore not be shocked when we experience them. The same applies to our mental life. The energy within is very volatile; it can erupt as anger or jealousy at any time and leave an impact. If we are aware of this then we can be prepared for all consequences, which follow us as tendencies from life after life. Ironically, we are full of pleasant expectations but are never ready for the unpleasant, and therefore continue to be shocked. Once we accept this as the normal state of affairs, then we can be aware of the primary desires, urges, and expectations, and the gravity of our reactions to them. The deeper the understanding, the greater would be our control on the oscillations of *sankalpa-vikalpa*. We have to always be ready for consequences.

Expectation is subconscious, and it is always there. We think of life as we lead it as "normal" or "natural." We take nature to be simple as well; however it is not so. The most difficult task for a human being to undertake is to control his or her mental energy. It is an extremely tough endeavour since it is working with subtle, volatile, and invisible energy. As lay people, we know of the physical energies to some extent, but we have no idea of the subtle energies that function within our system. Not realizing what we have undertaken, we expect that results should be easy to get. Our expectations make it all the more difficult to understand the nature of this energy. We become lax and passive, believing that this energy should function as per our expectations.

But "shoulds" do not always function according to our wishes. Therefore, either we understand the seriousness of controlling this energy as the starting point of our endeavour, or we will always remain dissatisfied. We do not actually know who the controller is and hence we assume that we are in charge, when we are not. Our tendencies make us function the way we do. These come from a deep past which we do not even believe in or accept. There was a time when people in India believed that this energy was difficult to control and therefore they listened with some faith to their teacher, or had faith in scriptural injunctions. Today we do not have that faith. We pay lip service that we believe in all these ideas, but we don't really have faith that functions. However, we can recover it through understanding.

The Reservoir of Tendencies

Where does sankalpa start? We really don't know. Our tendencies are very deep. These were not created in this lifetime. This concept itself is a problem. Do we understand that the consequences of our "wanting" to be born, or that our desire to enjoy objectivity, will influence the way we live our lives?

Let me explain objectivity. We believe that we are separate psychophysical beings, and that we are here to enjoy the "other" — be this in the form of an object, a relationship, or an activity. We first separate ourselves, and then we believe that we are here to enjoy without having to pay a price in the form of consequences, pleasant or unpleasant. We place anything or anyone that is outside this body in that objectivity. Having said that, the inner world of experience is also objectivity. How? Because our experience has to be separate from us for us to be conscious of it.

So we ask where does this objectivity start? It is almost

impossible to pinpoint unless we can understand our desire to enjoy. This desire is born with us, or is perhaps there before we are born. It is not something that we learn as we grow, in this lifetime. The learning is already there. Unless we take this into account, that we do not create this desire to enjoy only in this lifetime, how will we pinpoint it or get to the root of sankalpa? Again, it is not functioning only at the conscious level. In fact, it functions mostly at the subconscious level. We have already made the *sankalpa*; we have decided before our action, and connected to the purpose is the expected outcome! We do not take note of that which is started at the subconscious level. Taking note would imply reflection on what we do, why we do it, and how we do it.

These words — how, why, when, where — have been given to us as tools for reflection. They are used very precisely in science: when, exact date; where, exact place; how, exact process. But at the psychological level they are not limited just to this lifetime! Can we really handle the idea, with some faith, that we are not "new" persons? That we are very ancient? We find it almost impossible to believe that we could have had many lifetimes, many relationships, and the consequences are now following us. We look at the consequence; we get bothered; and then we ask, where did all this start?

Tracing the Path

There is a way to trace this path. Perhaps the simplest way is to look at our experience in this lifetime, follow the road we have walked so far, and reflect on the events that stand out in our memory. Then we can question and figure out why some events stand out while others are lost. But we pay more attention to those that stand out. And we do this, life after life, paying more attention to certain events or experiences. The consequences of those we can see now. When the consequences are pleasant we do not bother to reflect on them, but when they are unpleasant we want to question. While we can keep saying all this is not easy to understand, the purpose is not to take away the motivation. In fact, having undertaken this important task we need to work on it.

We have undertaken this human life as a consequence of tremendous tapasya. Whether this *tapasya* was conscious or subconscious, it doesn't really make a difference. We have the consequences in front of us now and we need to find out how it all started. We can find the answers because our entire past is present within us, right here and now. It hasn't gone anywhere. But do we want to follow that road which will show us how it all started, buried as it is in our unconscious and subconscious? We need to walk on the main highway, so to say. We need to enquire, which highway led us to this life? We can ask this question and look back and see that it is rooted in a tendency that we repeat, and without learning the lesson. We never start with a clean slate, and this is most difficult to accept.

There was a time when people accepted these ideas on faith, when they had simpler minds. They would listen to people in authority, or whom they trusted, and whatever was given to them as a method they followed. It was not even necessary that they understood the concept in depth, but with faith they accepted and followed, religiously. The belief that the idea was religious, sacred, or spiritual, meant that it was not questioned. The method was simply accepted as the one that would show the way.

Today that faith is completely missing. We are not even aware that we have lost faith. But if we realize that we have lost faith then we need some understanding to live by and move forward with. This is even more difficult.

For example, I talk of the law of consequence; what is this? It is the law of causation. And what is that? We can accept that physically we put a seed in the ground and under this law a tree or plant will grow. We also know that some soil, water, air, sunlight, fertilizer, or whatever, goes into making the plant or tree, and we immediately accept this as a "natural" outcome of the law of causation. But why should not the law of consequences, as applied to our lives, be equally natural? If the mind was to question and really understand, then it would try to make such thinking a part of its daily life and put it into action, without camouflaging its past.

If we camouflage the past then we do the same with the present as well. Our greatest folly is that we believe we are "in-charge" when actually we are not. How do we know? If we close our eyes here and now and observe what rises to the mind, we can come to know whether we are doing it or whether it is "being done." If the mental activity is involuntary, then we are not in charge! Therefore, the first step is to take responsibility. The more responsibility we take for this involuntary functioning, the deeper is our understanding — which then converts to a kind of control. We are not even in control of this physical system. It is an "automatic" functioning. Our conscious level is very weak, yet we consider it as absolutely powerful.

Talking of our tendencies as "good" and "bad" is again very difficult to sort out. While we are in the process, which is ongoing, there is the "good" and the "bad." But if we go deeper we realize that all our tendencies have a very powerful energy that gives us the deepest motivation. That energy in itself is neither good nor bad. When we try to utilize the energy, then the concepts of good and bad rise to the mind. We start with judgements, according to our backgrounds and our methods of processing. We have to watch how we use this energy. We have a fund of it, and if we want to use it for a particular purpose then we need to understand what the purpose itself is or could be.

This is where we bring in the judgement of "good" and "bad" as to what we have "learned." To begin, we need to "unlearn" the social norms that we find ourselves caught in and start afresh. The discrimination of whether our thoughts and actions are taking us towards freedom or not is what we need. As Vivekananda says, that which makes us strong takes us towards freedom.

On the other hand, we tend to follow a track which seems easier, even if we know it makes us weak. For example, there is the weakening search for immediate enjoyment or satiation of desires. Drugs, alcohol, etc., brings that immediate but temporary satisfaction. We may be aware of the consequence in terms of long-term misery, but we still go for these. The question is, can we exhaust the momentum of such tendencies? That is possible only if we can review the consequences in advance and then move forward. We will then have no cause for complaint or remorse, or even shock. Everyone experiments and makes mistakes but to face the consequences is a tall order. This is not a

matter of running away, or saying just for the sake of saying, "I don't want to enjoy and suffer." We would not be able to live a single day if we did not enjoy food; it's as basic as that! The very act of eating is an enjoyment. The very desire to exist is enjoyment. We have to look at our functioning, for every action is directed towards the desire for enjoyment.

What is Motivation?

Our motivation is connected to our emotions, which contain very volatile energy. If we do not camouflage the mind we can discover our obstacles. Sri Krishna points us to the stark reality in the *Bhagavad Gita*. If we want to live, that implies being ready to die at the same time. The moment we can accept the world as it is, we shall see the secret. When we perceive millions of people creating *sankalpa*, and millions complaining thereafter, then we will say, "Everyone does the same thing, *ad infinitum*," and ask ourselves, "So, for how long do we want to keep playing the same game?" We cannot lull ourselves into believing that we can remain untouched by consequences. As individuals in this psychophysical system, that is not possible.

Individuality is like a powerful nuclear force that keeps the center completely covered. Personality pulls whatever lies around it towards itself. This is the law of personality; it has tremendous magnetic force. We want to draw the entire universe towards ourselves. Each personality wants to "gobble up" the entire universe! This realization can motivate us to let go.

Freedom is the Goal

We have the desire to become free. As per the teachings of Advaita philosophy, this is the deepest and innermost desire of the human mind. Advaita says, we are free, but we believe we are bound. We have to base knowledge on faith. Then we can be persuaded that, if this is truth, then we can experiment with it. But are we ready to accept the very big challenge that deep within is a level that is already free?

In India, our ancient scriptures give us the Truth. Have we become so modernized that they do not apply to us? We are the same human beings with the same issues, problems, expectations, disappointments — everything is the same. We are those same non-thinking, error-prone human beings trying to be rational. We do not trust, we do not believe. The ancient rishis understood Truth, tried to solve these issues, and had nothing to hide.

Swami Vivekananda has stated that the quest for freedom is intrinsic to every human being. *"The people of old knew that fire lived in flint and in dry wood, but friction was necessary to call it out. So this fire of freedom and purity is the nature of every soul, and not a quality, because qualities can be acquired and therefore can be lost. The soul is one with Freedom, and the soul is one with Existence, and the soul is one with Knowledge."* If this is the Truth, then should we not make it our truth? The *Vedas* pay us the greatest compliment, stating; *"That Thou Art — You are Brahman."* But we are not ready to accept this! Why not? What stops us from accepting this grand compliment? The mind will respond to it as long as we do not try to somehow cover it up. The consequences of not accepting the truth lead us to bondage.

If we do have this innermost desire to be free, then let us look at our daily experiences. Do they give us freedom or place us in bondage? Actually, it is evident from our daily behavior that we do not believe we are free! What is this freedom? Is it the freedom from birth and death? Is it freedom from consequences? The answer lies in knowing that in reality we are free right now! I am not saying here that freedom implies not to feel or react; we are not stones! Freedom lies in acceptance. Life has to be understood, lived, and experienced through both suffering and enjoyment, but at the same time keeping the awareness that within us is the core of freedom which does not get affected in any way.

The Light of Awareness

Sankalpa is inevitable; understanding *sankalpa* is discrimination. Knowing the law of consequences is intelligence. It means being ready to expect and accept the consequences. The law of consequences means the law of reincarnation — acceptance of *samsara, punarjanma, karma*. We have lost faith; we are full of doubts which can only be cleared by understanding. We need to find that measuring tape of inner balance, and the next step will be the final one: practice. Once we clear our doubts and understand, then it is up to us to practice. Then we may take the path of *Nishkama karma* (action without desire for results), for that implies removing *sankalpa* altogether. It is easier, though, to accept the truth as demonstrated by those whom we believe in; then take up a method, practice, and gradually progress.

If we want control we need to identify at the deepest level. *"I Am the Light."* The more we emphasize That, the more we move away from objectivity and into control. Without the light of *Atman* nothing is available to us in terms of Truth. To emphasize the inner core, which is invisible, is very difficult. That is why religion gives us a divine image to place in our innermost core. That is the core of real control — knowing that we have this intrinsic reality, and the Light, our Light, is shining from that. This Light of Awareness will finally lead us to the desire to dissolve our individuality and merge into universality. The light we throw on experience is ours. Let us revive our Self-esteem and not continue to be covered by veils of ignorance. This is basic discrimination.

Pravrajika Vivekaprana, of the Ramakrishna Sarada Mission Order, is in-charge of the Ramakrishna Sarada Mission Retreat Centre in Pangot, District Nainital, India, in the foothills of the Himalaya. She has made a lifelong, in-depth study of Vedanta Philosophy and Hindu Psychology, as given by the ancient rishis of India, and as explained in contemporary terminology by the modern-day rishi, Swami Vivekananda. She has travelled widely, including the UK, Germany, Holland, South America, and the United States of America. Since 2006, her lectures have been published in the Understanding Vedanta Lecture Series, which are based on the study of various scriptures during regular study retreats, and through which she shares her thoughts on Vedanta with a much wider audience.

◆ SWAMI BRAHMESHANANDA

CODE OF CONDUCT
for Jain Householders

Although Jainism is a monastic oriented religion, the role of lay devotees is not underestimated. While the vows of laymen are only lighter versions of the *mahavratas*, meant to curb evil behaviors; on their own they cannot lead to final liberation. However, this point is not stressed. The Jain acharyas have realized that no institution can survive without the strong involvement of the laity. Hence they have shown high regard for this by producing numerous texts elaborating the lay conduct. Despite this trend, the ascetic orientation of Jainism is not lost, and even lay discipline is far more strict than in any other religious community. A Jain householder is called a *shravaka,* and the code of conduct is called *shravakachara.*

Like in any other major religion of the world, a person born in a Jain family is considered a Jain. Again, as in all major religions, a Jain by birth becomes a true Jain by the process of ritual initiation, which is something like baptism, and is called *samyakatva.* Yet, such a Jain, committed by faith alone, may not adhere to Jain precepts or follow the Jain way of life.

The code of conduct for a Jain householder (*shravakachara*) consists of: 1. Eight basic restraints or mula gunas; 2. Thirty five qualities of a noble life or *marganusari gunas;* 3. Twelve vows which include five *anuvratas, three guna vratas,* and four *shiksha vratas.* To these are added *sallekhana vrata,* and six essential duties. Their explanation follows:.

According to the *Digamber* sect of Jains, there are eight basic restraints called *mula-gunas* which a Jain householder must observe. They amount to refraining from taking meat, wine, honey, and five kinds of figs. The ingestion of these is prohibited because insects sometimes grow inside them. In lieu there are eight *mula gunas. Swetambaras* prescribe the avoidance of seven bad deeds, namely gambling, meat-eating, consuming alcohol, adultery, hunting, stealing, and debauchery.

Hemachandra, in his *Yogashastra,* has mentioned 35 qualities leading to a noble life. These are called the *marganusari gunas* of a Jain householder, found in ten verses, which have been rendered into English by Mrs. Stevenson in her book, *The Heart of Jainism,* and which are being quoted below.

1. He who gains his livelihood by honesty and admires and follows excellence of conduct, and marries his sons and daughters to well born and well behaved families.

2. He is afraid of committing sins; he follows the customs of his country; he never speaks evil of anyone, and especially not of his ruler.

3. He lives neither in too secluded nor too open a residence. It must be situated in a good locality and have good neighbors. The house must not have too many entrances.

4. He always associates with good men; he worships his parents and avoids an unprotected place of evil reputation. He does not indulge in evil actions.

5. He regulates his expenditure according to his income; he dresses according to his position, and being endowed with eight kinds of intelligence, he hears religious discourses every day.

6. If he suffers from indigestion, he limits his food. He eats only at fixed times. He gains his ends in such a way that one does not interfere with another.

7. He gives alms to those who come unexpectedly, to the sadhus, and to the poor; He is free from obstinacy and is partial to good qualities.

8. He knows his own strengths and weaknesses, and he avoids such actions as are not suited to the time and country in which he lives. He worships persons who are strict in keeping their vows and who are far advanced in knowledge; He feeds those who deserve feeding.

9. He is gracious; He has more than ordinary knowledge; He is grateful for what is done for him; He is loved by people; He is modest, merciful and of serene disposition; He is benevolent.

10. He is always intent on defeating the six interior enemies, and controls his five senses.

Such is the list of a householder's duties.

The Twelve Vows of the Jain Householder
Anu-vratas
1. Ahimsä. Sthulaprānätipāt-viraman-vrata - nonviolence
2. Satya. Sthula-mrushäväda-viraman vrata - truthfulness
3. Achaurya. Sthula- adattädäna-viraman vrata - nonstealing
4. Brahmacharya. Sva-därä-santosh vrata - celibacy
5. Aparigraha. Ichchhä-parimäna - nonpossessiveness

Guna vratas: Three merit or supporting vows
6. *Dig parimäna vrata* - restraints of geographical limits
7. *Desävakäsika Vrata* - strict geographical restrictions
8. *Anartha-danda-Vrata* - avoidance of purposeless activities

Shikshä vratas: Four disciplinary vows
9. *Sämäyika vrata* - practice of equanimity
10. *Bhoga upbhoga vrata* - consumption restraints
11. *Paushadha vrata* - practicing the life of a Monk
12. *Atithisamvibhäg-vrata* - discipline of share and care

1. Ahimsa Anuvrata is also called *Sthula-pränätipät-viraman-vrata,* or abstinence from gross violence. In order to steer clear of violence it is necessary to know the various ways in which violence is caused. It is of two kinds: (a) *Sankalpi* (intentional); and (b) *Ärambhi* (occupational). Hunting, offering animal sacrifice, killing for amusement, decoration, and sport are instances of intentional violence. Abstinence from those is possible without any great difficulty. All true Jains practice this type of non-violence.

Ärambhi-himsä is violence committed by a householder in the ordinary course of his life. It is of three kinds: (i) *Udyami,*

i.e. committed while undertaking some occupation in order to maintain oneself and one's family; (ii) *Gruhärambhi*, i.e., committed in carrying out the domestic acts like preparation of food, constructing home, cleaning, etc.; (iii) *Virodhi*, i.e., committed in self-defense or defense of one's property, members of one's family and friends, or the nation. However, aggression is strongly discouraged. One defends against thieves, robbers, dacoits, or enemies in battles. Jainism does not preach cowardice. Violence must not be indulged in out of hostility or revenge.

There are five transgressions (*Atichär*) of the vow of nonviolence:

1. Binding any creature or confining it harshly. 2. Beating and chasing animals. 3. Cutting the organs of animals or castrating them. 4. Making them carry heavy loads. 5. Withholding their food and drink

There are four attitudes here: Everyone should avoid violence and practice benevolence towards all living beings, feel joy at the sight of the virtuous, show compassion and sympathy towards the afflicted, and adopt an attitude of tolerance towards the insolent and ill behaved. Thus, the positive virtues which a votary of nonviolence must possess are: *Maitri* (love or friendship), *Pramoda* (joy and respect), *Karunä* (compassion), and *Mädhyastha* (tolerance or indifference) towards living beings.

2. Satya anu-vrata (truthfulness), also called *Sthula-mrushäväda-viraman vrata*, is abstinence from telling gross falsehoods. This also includes avoidance of harmful, rough, cruel or secret-revealing speech. It is falsehood to make a wrong statement through carelessness (*pramäda*). Gross falsehoods are those in which there is an evil intention combined with knowledge that the statement is false. According to Pujyapäda, that which causes pain and suffering to a living being is not commendable, whether it is according to the actual facts or not.

There are four kinds of falsehood: 1. Denying the existence of a thing with reference to its position, time, and nature, when it actually exists; 2. Assertion of the existence of a thing with reference to its position, time, and nature when it does not exist; 3. Where a thing is represented to be something different from what it actually is, and 4. When speech is ordinarily condemnable, sinful and disagreeable.

There are five transgressions of this vow:

1. Giving wrong advice about any matter and misleading people in matters of belief or conduct. 2. False accusations. 3. Disclosure of confidential matters, slandering others, talking about their weaknesses, and breaking a promise of secrecy. 4. Committing perjury or forgery, keeping false accounts, documents, and carrying on false propaganda about others; and 5. Committing breach of trust or misappropriation of what is entrusted to an individual in confidence.

3. Achaurya-Anu-vrata (nonstealing) is also called *Sthul-Adattädäna-Virman-vrata*, or taking what is not given freely. It is stealing when it is not granted by its owner (*swämiadatta*), when it is not granted by a living creature (*jivadatta*), when it is not granted by the *Tirthankars* (*jinadatta*), and when it is not given by the *Gurus* (*guruadatta*). In the modern context this vow of *Achaurya* would prohibit making illegal copies of software, unauthorized use of copyrighted material, and unauthorized downloading of music etc.

There are five transgressions of this vow:

1. Prompting someone to commit theft or showing him the way to commit theft. 2. Accepting or buying stolen goods without the real owner's consent. 3. Resorting to underhanded dealings against the rules that the state has imposed, like the smuggling of banned products, etc. 4. Using false weights and measures, such as heavier weights for purchasing articles while using lighter weights for the sale of one's own commodities. 5. Counterfeiting and adultery.

4. Brahmacharya anu-vrata (celibacy) is also called *Sva-därä-santosh* and *Para-stree-gaman-viraman-vrata*. It means to be content with one's legally married spouse and to desist from having sexual contact with other women.

There are five transgressions of this vow:

1. Arranging marriages of people other than one's own children, and celebrating the marriages of others. 2. Having sexual relation with a prostitute. 3. Having relations with a lady without a guardian present. 4. Having perverse or unnatural sex, or using unnatural means of sex gratification. 5. Having excessive sexual desire and heightened sex activity.

Thus a Jain householder must avoid any illicit sexual activities, must view a person of opposite sex as brother or sister, should not get involved in matchmaking except for his/her own children, and should not talk of lust or look at a person of opposite sex with lust.

5. Aparigraha anu-vrata (nonpossessiveness) is also called *Ichchhä Parimäna* or *Parigraha-Parimäna-vrata*. It means to set a limit to one's possessions and refrain from further acquisitions after one has what one needs. Every householder should impose upon him/herself restrictions as to the nature and extent of objects (animate and inanimate) so that there will be a check on possible greed or gluttony.

There are five transgressions of this vow:

1. Possessing land and houses, beyond the predetermined limit. 2. Possessing gold, silver and money more than the predetermined limit. 3. Keeping domestic articles like cattle, grains, and other provisions more than the predetermined limit. 4. Keeping servants, workers etc., beyond the predetermined limit. 5. Exceeding the limit of house-ware and equipment like utensils etc.

Three Guna-vrata (Supporting Restraints)

The three *Guna-vratas* — *Dig parimäna-vrata*, *Desävakäsika* and *Anartha-danda-vrata* — are intended to impose restraints of long duration on the activities of a householder, so that the chances of his committing transgressions of other vows is reduced. They are supplementary vows, which aid the individual in his observance of the *Anu-vrata*.

6. Dig parimäna-vrata (geographical restraints) means voluntarily limiting the area of one's activities. A householder vows not to travel beyond predetermined limits in all the ten directions. This helps him to curtail his activities so that his passions, particularly greed, can be curbed.

There are five transgressions of this vow:

1. Failing to limit the extent to which one can move upwards. 2. Failing to limit the extent to which one can move downwards (like into an underground chamber or into the deep-

er levels of the sea). 3. Travelling in any of the eight directions beyond one's fixed limits. 4. Extending the already set limits of one's travels. 5. Forgetting the set limits of one's travels and transgressing them.

7. Desävakäsika (Stricter geographical restrictions)

The basic idea underlying both the *Digvrata* and the *Desävakäsika Vrata* is that if a person restricts his movements, it will amount to keeping the *Mahä Vratas*, the rigid vows of an ascetic, in that safe and smaller area, and easier to manage. Besides, constant awareness of these spatial limits will result in increased vigilance in the observation of *Anu-vratas*. This vow requires an individual to determine and limit his movements to a house, a part of it, a village, or a town. The period for the observance of this vow may vary from a day to a few days, a month, a few months, or a year.

There are five transgressions of this vow:

1. Sending a message to someone beyond the fixed limit to do a required task. 2. Sending someone beyond the limit or getting work done by a servant already stationed outside. 3. Drawing the attention of others through signals or other gestures. 4. Revealing one's thoughts by secret looks or making sounds. 5. Revealing one's presence by throwing stones, etc.

8. Anartha-danda parimäna vrata (Avoidance of purposeless activities)

This vow prohibits the evils of purposeless inactivity due to idleness and negligence.

There are five transgressions of this vow:

1. Speaking indecent language which might provoke lust and infatuation in oneself or others. 2. Making indecent bodily gestures as might provoke laughter. 3. Shamefully indulging in meaningless talk and gossiping. 4. Giving articles which might be injurious to others for their use. 5. Hoarding articles of sense enjoyments such as garments, ornaments, scents etc., more than for one's basic requirements.

9. Sämäyika vrata (Forty eight minutes of meditation and equanimity)

This is a very important disciplinary vow (*Shikshä-vrata*). The practice of this vow consists in sitting quietly in a peaceful place for forty-eight minutes, without moving, calmly bearing cold, heat, mosquito bite, and other troubles, while maintaining perfect silence and control over the activities of body, mind, and speech. One should also meditate upon the transitory nature of the world, the true nature of the Self, on final Liberation, and should think as if he or she were a monk. Chanting holy texts, repenting misdoings, resolving not to repeat them, purging the mind of love and hatred towards all beings, and with complete equanimity, the keeper of this vow contemplates the principles that lead to self-realization. *Sämäyika*, if practiced regularly, brings about equanimity of mind and mental concentration, as well as successful abstinence from sinful activities. During the period of its practice, all kinds of attachments and proposed undertakings are absent, making it auspicious indeed.

There are five transgressions of this vow:

1. Performing unwholesome, improper, and undesirable bodily actions. 2. Speaking disagreeable and improper words. 3. Thinking wicked thoughts prompted by anger, envy, hatred, etc., while also thinking of the pros and cons of worldly matters. 4. Lack of interest in *Sämäyika* and inadvertence towards practicing it according to traditional formalities. 5. Forgetting about *Samayika*.

10. Paushadha Vrata (Practicing the life of a monk)

The tenth vow is the same as the ninth (*Sämäyika*), but is continued for twelve or twenty-four hours and accompanied by fasting. The word, *Prosadhopaväsa*, means fasting on the *Parva*, or a special religious day. It can be observed at home, in a forest, a temple, a monastery or at the *prosadha shälä* (hall for *prosadha*). One should pass the day as if he were a *sädhu*, in righteous contemplation, study of scriptures, and the adoration of the Jin, etc.,

> "Within the Samayika vrata vow, one should also meditate upon the transitory nature of the world, the true nature of the Self, on final Liberation, and should think as if he or she were a monk...." "....the keeper of this vow contemplates the principles that lead to self-realization."

and observe a 12 or 24-hour long *Sämäyika*. The intention is to get training so as to adopt that type of life whenever possible.

There are five transgressions of this vow:

1. Being careless in the act of evacuation and urination, doing so at a place where there might be insects etc. 2. Carelessness in placing and picking up objects. 3. Being careless in spreading of one's bedding. 4. Lack of zeal in careful observance. 5. Forgetfulness.

11. Bhoga-upabhoga parimäna vrata (restraints in all around consumption)

This vow enjoins the householder to restrict the use of objects used for *bhoga* and *upabhoga*. Bhoga items are those that can be used only once, such as food, soft drinks, lotions, perfumes, incense, etc. Upbhoga items mean those that can be used repeatedly, such as houses, furniture, clothes, shoes, jewelry, vehicles, etc. This latter, again, is of two kinds: *niyama* and *yama*. That which is undertaken for a limited time is called *niyama*, while the one which is undertaken for life is termed *yama*. To apply the vow, one can set the limitation of time for an hour, a day, a night, a fortnight, a month, a season, or a year. Renunciation of objects might fall around food, conveyances, beds, clothes, ornaments, cohabitation, music, and more.

There are five transgressions of this vow. These are mainly concerned with food, and include:

1. Eating green vegetables. 2. Eating fruits that contain seeds. 3. Consuming eatables mixed with living objects. 4. Consuming intoxicants. 5. Consuming something not properly cooked or difficult to digest.

In the modern context this vow consists of not accepting work in professions in which large scale violence is involved,

> "The Bhoga-upabhoga parimana vrata vow consists of not accepting work in professions in which large scale violence is involved, such as war, the burning of forests, and polluting of rivers and oceans, and the killing of animals for their flesh and furs."

such as war, the burning of forests, and polluting of rivers and oceans, and the killing of animals for their flesh and furs. Also, scrupulously avoiding food, drink, clothes, ornaments, utensils, whose production involves large scale violence is also enjoined, as well as limiting the quantity of those possessions whose production involves even a little violence.

12. **Atithi–samvibhäg-vrata** (Share and care discipline)

This vow consists of service and charity. It is also known as *Vaiyävruttya* or *Yathä Samvibhäg*. *Atithi Samvibhäg* literally means sharing with a guest, even with those who are unexpected and do not have a prior appointment. Monks and nuns, the poor, the destitute, and afflicted persons who might arrive unannounced, are really worthy persons to exercise this vow with.

There are five transgressions of this vow:

1. Placing food on a sentient thing (like the green leaf, or mixing food with sentient things). 2. Covering food with anything. 3. Saying that any object to be offered does not belong to the host, i.e., making an excuse for not offering it. 4. Lack of respect and veneration for monastics. 5. Not giving food and drink at the proper time.

Sanllekhanä-vrata (Death in a state of equanimity)

Apart from these twelve vows, a Jain householder is also expected to die a noble death in a state of equanimity. This is called *Sanllekhana*. Ideally it is a well-ordered, voluntarily chosen death which is not inspired by any passion, and in which the person, out of his own will, gradually gives up food in such a manner as would not disrupt one's inner peace and mindfulness. It is recommended only when the body is completely disabled by old age, or by incurable diseases, and the person becomes conscious of impending death and of the necessity of concentrating on the pure qualities of the soul.

For such an aspirant of this holy death, there is no dissatisfaction, no sorrow, no fear, no dejection, and no sinfulness present; the mind is calm and composed, and the heart is filled with the feeling of universal love and compassion. The aspirant slowly gives up solid food, then liquids, then water, and in the end observes a total fast with full resolve, fixing the mind on the holy *Navakär Mantra*. Thus, he peacefully and blissfully abandons the body.

There are five transgressions of this vow:

1. The desire to prolong life for fame of having endured a long *Sanllekhanä*. 2. A desire to die soon if passing becomes painful. 3. Having attachment for friends or sons, etc. 4. Keeping up the memory of past pleasures enjoyed. 5. A desire for sensory pleasures in the next life.

Essential duties, or *Avashyaka*

Along with these vows every Jain householder is ordinarily required to perform the following six daily duties:

1. *Deva puja*: Worship of the Arhats, the Adorables.
2. *Guru Bhakti*: Devotion to the guru, or the preceptor.
3. *Swadyaya*: Study of the scriptures.
4. *Samyama*: Control of mind and senses.
5. *Tapas*: Austerities such as meditation, fasting, etc.
6. *Dana*: Making charity of food, medicine, etc., to the needy.

In the *Swetambara* texts these six essentials are given differently, and are similar to those of monks.

Conclusion:

Jainism is one of the oldest religions of the world. These rules have grown and developed over centuries, being influenced by changing times and situations. An interesting and unusual feature in Jainism is the indepth descriptions of all the possible transgressions of the vows. These prove as guides for a sincere householder, and at the same time point to the presence of subtle deceptions in the mind.

How relevant are these rules in the modern times? Although times have changed, the human mind remains basically the same. There are more temptations now than before, though some may be of a different type. Whatever the case, a conscientious spiritual aspirant will find enough hints in these rules to guide him or her to lead a peaceful, noble, and exemplary life.

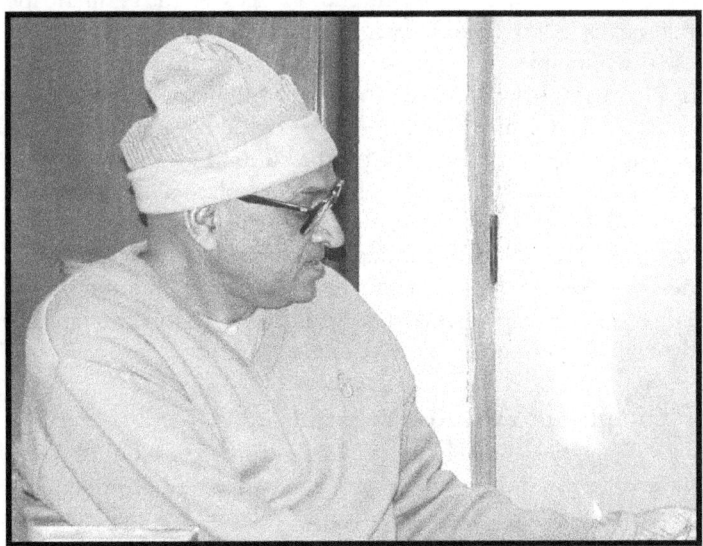

A former editor of the Vedanta Keshari, and previously of the Ramakrishna Mission Home of Service, Swami Brahmeshananda is a senior monk of the Ramakrishna Order and until recently was the Secretary of the Ramakrishna Mission Ashrama in Chandigarh, India. Over the years his writings in Hindi and English have appeared in several journals, including Prabuddha Bharata, Vedanta Kesari, and Nectar of Nondual Truth. He specializes in themes related to Jainism. He is now retired and is living in Varanasi.

◆ ANNAPURNA SARADA

AMERICAN IDEALS
Through the Crystal Clear Lens of Vedanta

Vedanta is in its 126th year in the United States, counting from Swami Vivekananda's advent at the 1893 Parliament of Religions in Chicago. In SRV Associations, we hold, in the open spirit of Sri Ramakrishna and Vivekananda, that there is no such thing as a foreign religion. All religions are indigenous to the Soul. Philosophically speaking, this is literally true according to the Seers in several world religions, since ultimately, there is but one Reality/God/Soul, and within That arises all concepts and phenomena. Relatively speaking, however, it is an Ideal to embrace both for one's own spiritual edification and for universal harmony. However, it is nondual philosophy, well-contemplated and well-practiced/applied, that will cause the distinctions between religions to first be understood and eventually be transcended.

The teachings of what the Indian Seers call *Sanatana Dharma*, Eternal Religion or Truth, are universal principles: realizable by persons living anywhere, at any time. When a religious or spiritual system of thought makes its way into a new region with a different cultural heritage, the principles of that system are what find resonance in the hearts of new adherents. We see that Swami Vivekananda emphasized principles over cultural expressions when he brought the Vedanta to the West. Authentic teachers of Vedanta do not seek to turn Americans, Europeans, South Americans, and others into Hindus; but rather, use the principles of Vedanta to awaken people from the bondage of identifying the Self with any kind of limitation, inclusive of bodies, culture, minds, and worlds. Along the way, the Vedantic principles throw a fresh light on the cultural ideals of a society. This is one way that Vedanta is taking its place and adjusting to each culture. Characteristically "American" traits or ideals such as self-reliance, individualism, egalitarianism, honesty and frankness, freedom, and others are revealed to be even more grand and noble – stepping stones to the Ultimate – when contemplated through the lens of Advaita Vedanta.

Principles of Advaita Vedanta

There are three basic principles that revolutionize one's view of life and all it contains. The first essential principle is that all Existence is One, specifically, "not two." All phenomena from the subatomic to the highest heaven belongs to one Reality that is eternal and unchanging. There are many schools of thought about what accounts for the diversity that we perceive, but the main point is that the Ultimate Reality is the single, ultimate Unit and that It is of the nature of pure Awareness. It is beyond the Witness and the objects witnessed; for It is "not two." Thus, it is also called "objectless Reality."

The second principle following from this is that there is only one Soul and we are all sharing It. The Ultimate Reality and the Soul, called *Atman* in Sanskrit, are identical. It is the source of the sense of "I" in all beings, "from the ant to the *Avatar*"; from the most basic life-form to *Ishvara*, the Personal God, the highest concept possible to the human mind. Thus, Consciousness is the same in all, only the manifestation is different, as Swami Vivekananda frequently stated, both from the nondual Vedanta scriptures as well as his own direct experience.

An important corollary of the first and second principles is that Reality/Soul/pure Awareness is all-pervasive. It permeates everything like physical space permeates objects, but It is dimensionless, being the substratum of all objects and dimensions, atomic, energetic, and conceptual. It is beyond the duality of gross and subtle, yet all that is gross and subtle, and even the void, exists in It.

The third principle is that the potential for everything – thought, energy, and matter – exists in that singular Ultimate Reality, and evolves outward into the world we experience via Mind: first Cosmic Mind, then collective mind, then individual mind, evolving out from subtle to gross. This means that all potential is in the Soul and the mind is the matrix of its manifestation as well as its dissolution via mental disciplines like meditation.

A final point here is that Vedanta is not a system of belief but one of realization. All these principles are the realization of countless seers and sages over millennia, even to our own time. They practiced spiritual disciplines like the teachers and seers before them, men and women both. Each person is to realize these directly, or they remain mere mental assertions. Hence, the formula is first to hear the truth, then contemplate and practice, and attain direct experience.

From this rarefied atmosphere of Advaita Vedanta's primary principles, we next look at how they inform our cherished cultural ideals and qualities. From the standpoint of human existence, we can rest assured that each one can be utilized to develop the kind of adamantine character needed for Self-Realization, which conduces to strengthening the spiritual life of ourselves and our communities.

Without the struggle towards the Infinite there can be no ideal.
    —Swami Vivekananda

Honesty & Frankness

Honesty is based on truthfulness and self-examination. To be honest is to relate facts as one understands them and to engage in self-examination to guard against a self-serving interpretation that amounts to lying to oneself, and which could

> "How can I be free of the whims of my desires and ego? What is always and ever true?" Answers to these questions require that one posits their sense of identity in the Soul, the true Self – a practice that begins with assuming the station of witness: witness of the given situation and of one's body, emotions, and thoughts that arise. This practice leads to the realization that the Soul/Self is not the body, mind, thoughts, intellect, or ego. These are objects seen by the witness, and clearly, the seer can never be the seen."

potentially hurt others by misrepresenting the truth of a situation. Frankness is part of this honesty, and is more specifically an American trait: a willingness to openly, truthfully state one's mind, even to those who are not well-known to us, and even to those who have some authority over us. It represents genuineness, friendliness, and safeguards the integrity of all concerned when engaged in responsibly at personal and community levels.

The practitioner of Vedanta looks at honesty in terms of its ultimate source and destination: absolute or non-dual Truth, another name for ultimate Reality. Non-dual Truth is changeless, but honesty is based upon an interpretation of facts, which can change due to time, place, and circumstances. It also changes as a result of the state of one's mind. The spiritual aspirant seeking a high level of veracity eventually asks, "How can I always know what is true in any given situation without fear that I will see it differently later? How can I be free of the whims of my desires and ego? What is always and ever true?" Answers to these questions require that one posits their sense of identity in the Soul, the true Self – a practice that begins with assuming the station of witness: witness of the given situation and of one's body, emotions, and thoughts that arise. This practice leads to the realization that the Soul/Self is not the body, mind, thoughts, intellect, or ego. These are objects seen by the witness, and clearly, the seer can never be the seen. One gradually ceases the conscious and unconscious "jockeying" for position relative to others. This egoic shifting of position is for self-preservation based on the false premise that "I am this psycho-physical being"; this alone prevents us from having a clear grasp of what is true in any given situation.

The goal of life according to Vedanta is to realize one's Self is indestructible; It is not born when the body is born and it does not die when the body dies. Thus, honesty and its self-examination makes a grand, subtle reorientation and links conventional honesty to ultimate Truth. In Sanskrit, we call this self-examination *Atma Vichara*, a practice that rests on discrimination (*viveka*) between the Self and the non-Self, and detachment (*vairagya*) from the non-Self. We no longer casually say, "I'm hungry," "I'm happy or sad," or "I did such and such or went somewhere." The true "I" is incapable of hunger and is omnipresent; it is the body that feels hunger, engages in activity, and goes from place to place; it is the mind that harbors emotions. We back up these conventional bits of communication with inner affirmation of what is really True. In this seemingly small way, honesty expands from moral and ethical incorruptibility to being a virtue that prepares us for the highest realization by weaning us off false identification from all that is not our true Self.

Individualism

This is an ideal or quality that most people probably take for granted as an American cultural trait without giving it much thought. It covers a wide scope of ideas from the state of being an individual, to different schools of political thought dealing with the right of the individual to freely act, create, seek their own destiny and happiness, and develop the best possible moral character.

In Swami Vivekananda's Jnana Yoga lectures, he calls on his audience to consider what makes us individuals. *"What is individuality? I should like to see it…If I lose one eye, or if I lose one of my hands, my individuality would be lost if it were in the body. Then, a drunkard should not give up drinking because he would lose his individuality…. No man ought to change his habits for fear of this. There is no individuality except in the Infinite. That is the only condition which does not change. Everything else is in a constant state of flux… . We are not individuals yet. We are struggling towards individuality, and that is the Infinite, that is the real nature of man. He alone lives whose life is in the whole universe, and the more we concentrate our lives on limited things, the faster we go towards death."* – Complete Works of Swami Vivekananda (CW) 2:80-81

What does this mean for our being individualists in practice? If our destiny is to realize our true individuality as ultimate Reality, then the goal of individualism becomes to manifest that Reality in all we think and do. Far from cultivating the possibility for narcissism, greed for wealth, domination, and disdain for the good of others that an ego-driven individualism can, spiritualized individualism relinquishes the sense of ownership and agency with regard to the intelligence, creativity, genius, and energy/action manifesting through one's mind and body. Mind and body are not their source; Reality, our true Individuality, is their Source. The problems of selfishness – pride, possessiveness, jealousy, anger, hatred, etc. – disappear for good when this is clearly understood.

Egalitarianism

This wonderful ideal links easily to the last, for, if individualism extols the value of the individual, egalitarianism expresses the same idea collectively – that all people are equal and should have equal opportunity. This ideal often fails in practice, as we know. This is due to seeing the cause of equality in the physical only. The brother/sisterhood of human beings is

> "Disciplining ourselves to see through the appearances of male, female, race, age, religion, personalities, physical and mental disabilities, is a spiritual path of its own leading to the rare and exalted virtue of same-sightedness that we saw in Buddha, Christ, and others. In Sanskrit, it is called *samadarshitvam*."

generally seen as based on all of us having a human body, or all of us living on the same planet. Many who believe in the existence of a soul, have not actually seen it distinct from the body, i.e. the body still makes one soul different from the other. Vedanta explains the true basis of this equality: there is but one Self/Soul, and all these psycho-physical coverings called bodies (and not just human bodies at that) are sharing It. Our intrinsic equality is more truly based on the indivisible Self manifesting in all beings. Disciplining ourselves to see through the appearances of male, female, race, age, religion, personalities, physical and mental disabilities, is a spiritual path of its own leading to the rare and exalted virtue of same-sightedness that we saw in Buddha, Christ, and others. In Sanskrit, it is called *samadarshitvam*. Beyond that is the realization "I am the Self in all," or, as Jesus said, "I am the Light of the world."

Self-Reliance & Independence

We place a premium on being independent. In economically favorable times young adults expect to live separately and not depend on parents. We admire those who make their way and solve their own problems by hard work, sacrifice, and perseverance. Harnessing these noble traits for the attainment of Self-realization is a powerful practice. Generally, self-reliance means depending upon the powers of the body and the mind, believing all the while "I am the body and the senses and they are mine." Reliance on the psycho-physical being as the source of one's identity, strength, creativity, and ingenuity is a limitation, from the Vedantic view. We cannot be truly independent or free so long as we are dependent upon anything that changes. This is a profound shift, to go from ordinary self-reliance to Self-reliance, from dependence on the shifting sands of mind and body, to the independence of knowing oneself as the Source of all strength and creativity. Aligning oneself with Infinite Being increases one's stamina, patience, and perseverance.

Freedom

This word is a cultural touchstone for Americans. The Founders of the U.S. were intent on creating a society of religious, political, economic, and personal freedom. According to Vedanta, these represent relative freedom. If one's freedom is only based on these, then it can be taken away. Further, if we are fortunate enough to have all these relative freedoms, are we still free? If we look closely, we will see that we are dragged here and there by attachments and aversions arising from the mind and body. Are we really free to simply sit still for as long as we wish? Eventually hunger and thirst make us move, if not the demands of work and family. Are we free to concentrate our mind on a single topic, earthly or spiritual, whenever we like? In most cases, no. The busy mind throws up a myriad other topics, desires, and aversions for distraction. So, although a part of us feels free, the body, mind, elements – internal and external nature – are showing us that we are not. This is the fundamental suffering in life caused by taking the body and mind to be the Self, what Vedanta terms root ignorance.

The Seers of India, including Lord Buddha, sought to overcome internal and external nature by disciplining the mind to trace the source of the sense of "I" and the origin of our sense of freedom. Transcending identification with body, senses, energy, and the highest reaches of mind through deep concentration, they realized the inherent Freedom of the Soul, *Moksha*, a Freedom that is ever at hand, is our very nature, and which can never be taken away. How can the birthless, deathless Soul be bound by anything? It is infinite and all-pervasive. When one logically examines that statement, it becomes clear that Eternal Truth, ultimate Reality, Existence, pure Awareness, true Freedom, Soul, Self, The Individual – all these describe the same Reality. There can only be one "infinite"; for, if there were two, they would limit each other and therefore not be free.

A Return to Tradition

While making this selection of ideals to write about, drawn primarily from my own upbringing in a white, middle class, West Coast, Catholic family, I happened across other lists of qualities from the early days of the United States. Among them were three that did not get transmitted to me from my upbringing or schooling as ideals, but which should have been foremost: self-control, education, and wisdom. I only hope they would appear on others' lists of current American ideals. Vedanta has much to say about these.

Self-Control

The pendulum may sometimes swing away from self-control as it has in recent decades, but it must always swing back because lack of self-control results, eventually, in terrible suffering. Swami Aseshanandaji stated frequently from the podium of the Portland Vedanta Society, "We don't want freedom to the senses, but freedom from the senses!" Vedanta and Yoga Psychology clearly delineate the connection between the indulgent use of the senses for pleasure and the draining of the body and mind of vital energy, leaving them in a weakened state for dealing with the karma that accrues from selfish acts. Emotionalism, brooding, depression – all of these follow the habitually indiscriminate and wasteful use of the mind and senses. It is interesting to note that even in the U.S., until recently, unmarried persons were expected to remain celibate until marriage. Unfortunately, only religious and social reason are generally cited, which do not speak to the far-reaching benefits to individuals and society that conservation and sublimation of sexual energy in youth has on

the development of memory, concentration, and will power. Sublimation, here, is the essential point and one that seems to have gotten confused with and replaced by repressive approaches, thereby causing the pendulum to swing reactively to undisciplined, egoic self-expression. Again, when one takes the body and mind as the Self, then the immature ego romps in the playground of the six passions. We have to realize that self-control, which means being in control of the mind and senses instead of under their control, leads to peace and contentment, which are the prerequisites for realization of the Self.

Education

In my experience, we have grown accustomed to thinking that the primary if not the sole aim of public education and higher education to be the training of a national workforce. Meanwhile, some bemoan the loss of a well-rounded education that elevates the mind and character as careers become ever more specialized and technological and large numbers of students lean toward those subjects that promise the greatest financial reward. Completely "outside the box" are the ideas of Vedanta with regard to knowledge and education, which begin with reverence for the divine nature of education. Synthesizing the teachings of several schools of India's philosophical thought and expressing them for the modern era, Swami Vivekananda famously stated: *"Education is the manifestation of the perfection already in Man."* (*Letters of Swami Vivekananda*, pg. 70)

One of the first teachings in Vedantic thought is that all knowledge lies within. The perfection the swami refers to is that pure Awareness in which lies the potential for all knowledge. All manifestation begins as an idea in the mind – Cosmic Mind, collective, and individual – moving from potential, to subtle or conceptual form, to physical form through those three phases of mind. When we learn something, as Vivekananda explains in Karma Yoga, it is not outside, but inside. *"The external world is simply the suggestion, the occasion, which sets you to study your own mind, but the object of your study is always your own mind. The falling of an apple gave the suggestion to Newton, and he studied his own mind. He rearranged all the previous links of thought in his mind and discovered a new link among them, which we call the law of gravitation."* (CW 1:28)

The role of the teacher in this case is to remove the obstacles in the way of discovery. Guiding children in the acquisition of concentration is paramount, as is the ability of parents and teachers to recognize negative samskaras, inherent tendencies or impulse, that impede the child. These are naturally addressed through training in virtues like nonviolence, truthfulness, self-control, and contentment, along with surrender to God and study of the revealed scriptures, i.e., those scriptures that talk about the nature of the individual soul and its relation to ultimate Reality.

Wisdom

Wisdom was held in high esteem during the time of the country's founding. Whether it was perceived as an earthly or spiritual faculty, it seems today that wisdom has become confused with knowledge, and knowledge confused with information. Vedanta makes a distinction between lower and higher knowledge. Lower knowledge concerns knowledge of earthly things: arts, literature, language, history, sciences, vocations, etc. Higher knowledge refers to either the knowledge that leads to Self-Realization or to Self-Realization itself. In this discussion we use it in both senses. Both lower and higher knowledge are considered sacred since they both emanate from the same ultimate Reality. The purpose of lower knowledge is for one's earthly benefit, which should ultimately serve to aid the individual to concentrate and realize the higher Knowledge, Freedom/Moksha.

With this perspective in mind, let us return to what appears as today's confusion between wisdom, knowledge, and information. In the sphere of lower knowledge: Information consists of facts or data that one may or may not know how to connect for any useful benefit. To be knowledgeable is to have a deep understanding of a particular subject or subjects via concentrated study. (Lower) knowledge no doubt guides us with regard to living our lives and understanding the world, but it is still confined to the realm of the more or less refined ego and its tendency toward possessiveness and power as discussed in the section on Individualism. In the sphere of higher Knowledge: Wisdom, according to Yoga and Vedanta, is the direct experience of knowledge. In Yoga, we would say that the yogi has performed *samyama* on some facet of knowledge – concentration, meditation, and absorption – and arrived at its Essence. In Vedanta, we would say that knower, knowledge, and act of knowing have been unified. It is in this state, transcending Mind and its three phases, that one discovers that all knowledge lies within, that education/knowledge is the "manifestation of the Perfection" already in the Soul. Wisdom, therefore, transcends knowledge, yet never contradicts it. It is superior to conventional thinking and knowledge, which are limited to time, place, and circumstance. Wisdom is founded on ultimate Truth, thus those who have attained to it are the revered guides of humanity.

Annapurna Sarada is the president of SRV Associations and an assistant teacher for the sangha members and their children. She also writes a blog for Advaita-Academy.org. To read more about SRV's children's classes and retreats, visit the newsletter archive on SRV's website: www.srv.org

◆ SRV ASSOCIATIONS

RETURN TO THE SANCTITY OF CHILDBIRTH
An Ardent Appeal by Illumined Monk and Ancient Lawgiver

In January and February of 1900, Swami Vivekananda delivered seven lectures to the Shakespeare Club of Pasadena in California, comprised primarily of women. From one of his lectures, *"Women of India,"* are to be found some stark and revealing statements of the Great Swami on the principle of sacred childbirth in India. We can expect that the women of 1900 he spoke to followed the stricter rules of American and Christian society of those days compared to our own contemporary society. The ideas he expressed, undoubtedly poignant then, are even more so today. Vivekananda carefully prepared his audience to hear these perhaps shocking ideas from India with an open mind and distill from them essential principles to recast a future society in our own times.

In this essay appear commentaries on these statements by Swami Vivekananda concerning motherhood, fatherhood, and childbirth which are crucial of consideration in sight of two developments in our Westernized societies. First, that giving birth to children today is rarely a thoughtful and conscious act but a biological process that the forces of materialism have stripped of any sense of reverence or sensitivity for the soul that is incarnating; secondly, that the vast majority of parents who do plan and prepare for childbirth are really lacking any knowledge of the dynamics of the soul's condition prior to birth, the circumstances of its advent on earth, and the qualities, characteristics, and *karmas* that this being is bringing into manifestation.

The expression today, "planned parenthood," is really a misnomer, then, since any aspirations for the child's birth and life on earth on the part of the expectant parents are grossly limited to its existence as a body only. The incarnating soul's actual spiritual status, i.e., its true, stainless nature as pure, conscious Awareness, gets overlooked as does the Eternal Home from which it will emerge, and to which it will (hopefully) return at the end of its life on earth.

The profound words of Swami Vivekananda, shown in italics below, reflect both a higher vision and a better time for the presently beleaguered principle of child-bearing and child-rearing, all pertinent to this plane of existence. Forethought around the child's spiritual future and well-being was preeminent in the minds of ancient Aryan parents, and "planning" for their future meant protecting the child against not just the dangers of the external world and nature, but more importantly, protecting its relationship with Brahman and the precious knowledge of its ever pure and perfect Soul, the *Atman*.

Only a spiritual life can both protect and provide in this especial way, and ensure that the unacceptable insinuation of *avidya*, forgetfulness of one's Divine Nature, will never plague the soul during its temporary sojourn in the fields of name and form. This dangerous amnesia of the soul, the "Spiritual Alzheimer's Disease" of our time, is to be resisted at all costs. All else, all the other many plagues and problems of relative existence, will occur anyway in space over time. But they will become lessons resulting in great strength for the soul that is in memory of its Divine Heritage, while for the forgetful soul, these very trials will turn into *karmas* and *samskaras* (habits persisting over lifetimes) that will pull it back and down into rebirth again and again in *samsara* (rounds of birth and death in ignorance). Parents raised in the perennial *dharma* over lifetimes by conscious parents of their own are aware of this.

This set of esoteric facts concerning the phenomena of birth and rebirth, whether conscious or unconscious, is even more powerful in view of one superior saving grace. This is, that perfect or near perfect beings are also awaiting rebirth on earth in order to benefit and free mankind, and conscious/*dharmic* and sensitive would-be parents are highly desirous of receiving such rare souls as their loving caretakers. This is a good juncture to enter into the Great Swami's words on the subject, followed in each case by some helpful commentary, and some quotes from Lord Manu's scripture, *The Code of Ethics*, mentioned by Vivekananda below. These will help to give the reader an idea of the profound importance that the ancient Aryans placed on the conception of their children. Moreover, such statements from ancient scripture might go a long way in influencing parents of this day and time towards performing austerities and purifications, long before the actual inception of the child, thus filling the criteria for receiving illumined souls into their families here on earth.

Scriptures and The Mother

"The Ramayana and Mahabharata have been the cherished heritage of the whole Hindu world for the last several thousands of years and form the basis of their thoughts and of their moral and ethical ideas. In fact, the Ramayana and the Mahabharata are the two encyclopedias of the ancient Aryan life and wisdom, portraying an ideal civilization which humanity has yet to aspire after." (The Complete Works of Swami Vivekananda, hereafter "CW", 4:100)

"Now, the ideal woman in India is the mother, the mother first, and the mother last. The word woman calls up to the mind of the Hindu, motherhood; and God is called Mother." (CW vol. 8, "Women of India")

"In the West, the woman is wife. The idea of womanhood is concentrated there – as the wife. To the ordinary man in India, the whole force of womanhood is concentrated in motherhood. In the Western home the wife rules. In an Indian home the mother rules." (CW ibid.)

"Is woman a name to be coupled with the physical body only? Ay! The Hindu mind fears all those ideals which say that the flesh must cling unto the flesh. No, no! Woman! Thou shalt not be coupled with anything connected with the flesh. The name has been called holy once and forever, for what name is there which no lust can ever approach, no carnality ever come near, than the one word mother? That is the ideal in India." (CW ibid.)

"The ideal of womanhood in India is motherhood – that marvelous, unselfish, all-suffering, ever-forgiving mother." (CW ibid.)

This Great Swami was also the one who stated that there

could be no resurrection for India, or for the world, unless woman be raised to her natural and elevated status once more — as in the ancient days when women *rishis* (seers) such as Gargi, Maitreyi, and Lopamudra were living and teaching.

Pray for Divine Offspring

"*According to the Hindu mind, is the great mission of woman – to become a mother. But oh, how different! Oh, how different! My father and mother fasted and prayed, for years and years, so that I would be born. They pray for every child before it is born. Says our great lawgiver, Manu, giving the definition of an Aryan, 'He is the Aryan, who is born through prayer.' The child must be prayed for.*" (CW ibid.) Vivekananda states that "*....those children that come with curses, that slip into the world, just in a moment of inadvertence, because that could not be prevented*" enter the world with a tremendous disadvantage that exacerbates their *karmas* and *samskaras*.

As *The Code of Manu* points out: "*A man of bad conduct, devoid of sacred rites, is blamed among people; he constantly suffers misfortunes, is afflicted with diseases, and is short-lived, and his offspring are like him.*" Those of bad conduct create a web of negative karmas responsible for a multitude of personal and familial calamities over generations. Without those disciplines ("sacred rites" and spiritual practices) that neutralize *karmas* and render one's mind peaceful and life balanced, the soul draws to itself other souls of similar character over successive lifetimes.

What further and living proof do we have, or do we need, than an example like this Great Swami, whose parents were more than just pious; they were spiritually-oriented. And concerning proof, again, what more do we need than the haunting and telling specter of the multitude of ignorant souls being born on earth today, all caught up in the regime of maya, engaged in mindlessness money-making and malicious acts of violence and war. Even today's vaunted moral life is tinged with the ills of dishonest politics, shady business dealings, fundamentalist religious narrowness, and attachment to surface pleasures. Even if the child is of relatively good mind, life in the tepid admixture of such worldliness may soon render it crooked and wayward.

Marriage, Education, and Families

"*Do you all pray for the children to come? Are you thankful to be mothers, or not? Do you think that you are sanctified by motherhood, or not? Ask that of your minds. If you do not, your marriage is a lie, your womanhood is false, your education is superstition, and your children, if they come without prayer, will prove a curse to humanity.*" The ancient ideal in India taught that children were for the benefit of society, not the pleasure or security of the parents. Thus, it was incumbent on the would-be mother and father to protect the entire process of bringing forth and raising children. It was a sacred responsibility that penetrated every other social institution. Asking American women in 1900 to examine the basis of their marriage, their education, and their own view of themselves as mothers or potential mothers must have been exhilarating and eye-opening for them. Shall we ask ourselves today? What is the goal of marriage, of education? When we plan to have children, is it for our pleasure? Do we raise them with their own ultimate good and the greater good of society in mind? Do we feel sanctified by this process?

Here, an expansion of the meaning of the way that Swamiji uses the word "prayer" would be helpful. For, prayer without purification and spiritual disciplines is, as most beings have found out, totally ineffective — both for eliciting any answer from the Divine, or for getting one's desires duly granted. Further, prayer is really a matter of the past rather than the future. All that the human being has prayed for over lifetimes is granted at the beginning of his or her next life. In other words,

you have been granted all that you wanted. Your present lifetime is for utilizing those boons for your own fulfilment, and that of others. Those who go about this task wisely will finish up their works on earth and gain that unique higher wisdom (*jnanam*) that will merge them into Peace and Bliss thereafter. Others will find themselves repeating their old mistakes, praying futilely for help and goods that are already manifest in their lives. This is the difference between wisdom and ignorance in embodied souls.

More pertinent to Swamiji's terse warnings above, again, proof is not wanting. "*Fair faces and false hearts,*" as he stated, are common and running rampant among both sexes today; both true manhood and womanhood are at a premium. And how many hopeful youths have had their expectations dashed in life after gaining what Sri Ramakrishna called a "*mere bread-winning education*" advised and forced by the world societies, both Eastern and Western, upon them?

And finally, there are so many of those poor examples of humanity, called "our children" in modern times, proceeding from loveless marriages where selfishness reigns supreme. They are thus willing to easily cast away the parents who raised them and take the fortunes they have gathered without a second thought, and with no thought of gratitude or sense of reciprocal service whatsoever in mind. Both sides, the selfish parents and greedy youths, retell a story of suffering and *karmas* accrued, sending all involved into a samsaric hell of their own devising. *The Code of Manu*, in contrast, extols spiritual, consecrated unions and their noble offspring (*dharmic* families) that can liberate not only parents and children, but confer blessings on ancestors and descendants:

"*Listen, ye Brahmanas, while I fully declare what quality has been ascribed by Manu to all marriage-rites. The son of a wife wedded according to the Brahma rite, if he performs meritorious acts, liberates from sin ten ancestors, ten descendants, and himself as the twenty-*

first. The son born of a wife, wedded according to the Daiva rite, saves seven ancestors and seven descendants. The son of a wife married by the Arsha rite saves three ancestors in the ascending and descending lines, and the son of a wife married by the rite of Prajapati saves six in either line. From the four marriages here enumerated beginning with the Brahma rite, children radiant with knowledge of the Vedas and honored by the Sishtas (good men) spring forth)."

Discipline and Purification Prior to Pregnancy

"….*Our books teach that it is the pre-natal influence* [even before conception] *that gives the impetus to the child for good or evil. Go to a hundred thousand colleges, read a million books, associate with all the learned men of the world — better off you are when born with the right stamp…. We come with a tremendous impetus for good or evil… born demons or born gods. Education or other things are* [of little consequence]. *Thus say our books: direct the pre-natal influence.*" (CW ibid.)

"*She was a saint to bring me into the world; she kept her body pure, her mind pure, her food pure, her clothes pure, her imagination pure, for years, because I would be born. Because she did that, she deserves worship.*" (CW ibid.)

"*Why should mother be worshipped so much? Because she made herself pure. She underwent harsh penances sometimes to keep herself as pure as purity can be. For, mind you, no woman in India thinks of giving up her body to any man; it is her own. When a man comes in physical contact with his wife, the circumstances she controls through what prayers and through what vows! For that which brings forth the child is the holiest symbol of God himself. It is the greatest prayer between man and wife, the prayer that is going to bring into the world another soul fraught with a tremendous power for good or for evil. Is it a joke? Is it a simple nervous satisfaction? Is it a brute enjoyment of the body? Says the Hindu: 'no, a thousand times, no!'*"

The Shining Example of These, and all Times

Calling back the fading but still present idea of true motherhood to mind, our Great Swami couples it most naturally with the ideal of purity. He, himself, saw with his own eyes the perfect woman, perfect wife, and perfect mother, in Sri Sarada Devi, his *guru's* incomparable wife and spiritual consort, so he was well aware of what the Ideal looked like and epitomized. She is, as well, the example of universal Motherhood that transcends the focus on body-born children and creates mind-born children. It is only a pure and powerful receptacle such as the pure woman that can be the fit vehicle for illumined souls who emanate from inner worlds much more light-filled than this one, manned with a divine purpose that will benefit, not hamper, the growth and evolution of souls caught there, or seeking freedom. About preliminary rites, rituals, and practices that precede even the conception of the child itself, *The Code of Manu* declares:

"*By the study of the Vedas, by vows, by burnt oblations, by the recitation of sacred texts, by acquisition of the threefold sacred sciences, by offerings made to the gods, rishis, and manes, by the great sacrifices, and by sacred Srauta rites, this human body is made fit for the procreation of blessed children, and also for union with Brahman.*"

We have learned from some of the superlative beings who made their way out to the physical plane of existence that in the subtle realms all souls are born of the mind, the parents using the condensed force of mental concentration fused with their own realizations in spiritual life and practice. Why should it not be the same here on the physical plane, that parents use the force of concentration for conscious childbirth, as taught in *Yoga*, for instance — especially given that there are some shining examples of illumined parents and their bright and intelligent offspring already present in the history of this planet, even manifesting recently in our own times. *The Code of Manu* expresses these powerful abilities and processes:

"*Through virtuous conduct one obtains long life, through virtuous conduct desirable offspring, through virtuous conduct imperishable wealth. Virtuous conduct destroys the effect of inauspicious markings in them and their offspring. In addition to this, a whole series of austerities and ceremonies must be performed by future parents in order to sanctify the body and make it ready for receiving the unborn soul, all at the proper time and in the proper order.*"

Put in more blatant terms, should the conception and production of something so divine as a child be left, as Swami Vivekananda states, to "*brute enjoyment*" or a moment of simple "*nervous satisfaction?*" If it is, the result will be the appearance in one's arms of a soul-baby who has been drawn straight from the ocean of suffering and confusion (*samsara sagara*) rather than emanating directly from the ocean of Peace and Bliss (*ananda sagara*). It is the parents and their quality of consciousness who set themselves up for this, or let themselves in for it — as the case may be.

The Sacred Seed and the Fertile Soil

All of this talk and teaching pertinent to the motherhood of God, and to the important role and sanctity of women, is not meant to either underplay the role of the father or let him off the hook regarding his own need for personal practice of disciplines and purifications. *The Code of Manu* explains this:

"*According to sacred tradition, woman is declared to be the soil, and man is declared to be the seed; the production of all corporeal beings takes place through the union of the soil with the seed, so the parents ought to prepare themselves for good offspring in advance via spiritual austerities performed by them both, individually and together. It should be understood in advance, that in some cases the seed is more distinguished, and in some the womb of the female is more so, but when both are equal, the offspring is most highly esteemed.*"

This teaching of inherent characteristics in the seed of the human male points to the need for him to purify both his body and its seed, and to preserve that seed (semen/*sukla*) as inward power as well. Put directly, before he impregnates his wife with his seed, he must impregnate his seed with divine qualities and power drawn from his own intense practices and austerities.

In the interim of this now sanctified process, since both the father's semen and the mother's egg are produced by food, it is well to keep in mind this teaching of Sri Sarada Devi, the Holy Mother: "*From pure food comes pure blood; from pure blood proceeds pure energy (prana). From pure energy comes pure thought, and from that all-important principle comes pure mind. Pure mind is God.*" This sublimation process, the knowledge of which is almost entirely missing in this day and age, can only be gotten via the method of divine recollection that proceeds from training under an illumined preceptor, study of revealed scriptures, and contemplation and meditation upon Truth Eternal.

NECTAR BOOK REVIEWS

Josephine MacLeod and Swami Vivekananda's Mission
by Linda Prugh (forward by Swami Chetanananda)
Published by Sri Ramakrishna Math, Chennai
Paperback, 543 pgs, illustrated

"The new cycle must see the masses living Vedanta and this will have to come through women."
– Swami Vivekananda, Inspired Talks, p. 195

Josephine Macleod (1858 – 1949), an American woman of unforgettable and noble character, played an enormous role in Swami Vivekananda's mission. His mission included spreading the universal teachings of Advaita Vedanta in the West, saving his countrymen (India) from poverty and ignorance by re-awakening them to the "man-making" spirituality of their own great Seers, and establishing the Ramakrishna Order of monks. From the time Josephine met Vivekananda in 1895 at a class in New York City, and until her own passing, she spent the greater part of those 54 years doing everything she could to help fulfill that mission in the West and India during his lifetime and after.

Preparing the reader for Josephine's first encounter with Vivekananda, the author writes, "Joe MacLeod was not looking for toys. ...She was not looking for powers. ...She was not looking for love. ...As her niece, Frances Leggett stated, 'Joe wanted only the real and the earnest.'" About that first meeting, Josephine explained: "Meeting Swamiji changed my life in a twinkling! But I was ready – the readiness is all." And "...from that hour, life had another purpose, because it gave that strength that's within one – not what is without." Independent by nature, with an indomitable will, she was described by Vivekananda as one who could "wield a kingdom," and who would be "great without the help of any man."

Early in her life she developed a passion for simplicity and spontaneity such that she could pack and catch a steamer ship in a matter of hours and be gone for months or even years. Traveling from place to place most of her life she cultivated relationships with some important people of her day. Echoing a favorite statement of Vivekananda's that every day he learned, she would frequently state that her religion was "to learn." Freedom, commitment to Truth, and the ability to give, serve, and to love without expecting anything in return were also hallmarks of her character. She imbibed Vivekananda's unwavering stand within the boundless Self and the Truth, Freedom, and Peace that flows from that. Of Swamiji she once said, "The thing that held me ... was his unlimitedness! I never could touch the bottom – or top – or sides!"

Josephine MacLeod and Vivekananda's Mission presents Josephine's life with a myriad living details that will acquaint and fascinate the reader with this fearless soul. The voluminous amount of research by the author, coupled with empathy, insight, and great writing has rendered this historical narrative into a "page turner" covering the lives of dynamic, intellectual Western women at the turn of the last century whose lives were entwined with hers – women who embodied the qualities of intelligence, curiosity, open-mindedness, a passion for truth, commitment to high Ideals, sacrifice, and service. Josephine MacLeod served Vivekananda's mission by connecting him, before and after his passing in 1902, with influential men and women who could be of help. She stayed in communication with the great thinkers, artists, writers, scientists, European nobility, and government officials of those days. Josephine was behind the many translations and publications of Vivekananda's works during her lifetime, biographies on him and Sri Ramakrishna that generated a new wave of interest leading to at least two international Vedanta Societies, and aided the Ramakrishna Order with her diplomacy during the turbulent times of Britain's colonial rule. To read a list of the people she brought to Vivekananda or to his teachings reads like a who's who of late 19th and early 20th centuries. As a result, the author necessarily read and digested innumerable letters, articles, and books of and about these persons in writing this book. The bibliography is pages long and well worth reading.

From the back cover of the book:

"It is the 'truth' that I saw in Swamiji that has set me 'free.' One's faults seem so insignificant. Why remember them, when one has the Ocean of Truth to be one's playground?"
– Josephine MacLeod

Mother of Mayavati
The Story of Charlotte Sevier and Advaita Ashrama
By Amrita M. Salm Ph.D.
Advaita Ashrama, 2013,
399 pages

This well-researched and engaging biography tells the story of Charlotte Sevier, a British disciple of Swami Vivekananda, who left the security and comforts of Victorian England to fulfill her guru's vision of an ashram in the Himalayas devoted to the practice of Advaita Vedanta. She and her husband, Captain Sevier, sold all they had and accompanied Vivekananda on his triumphant return to India after nearly four years in the West. They purchased a parcel of land in the Himalayan foothills that became a center for training Indian monks to teach in the West, and also served as a training ground and retreat for Western Vedantists working in India. Thus, East and West worked and practiced together.

Advaita Ashrama immediately became the new home of Prabuddha Bharata, (Awakened India) the English language journal of the Ramakrishna Order for disseminating the universal teachings of Vedanta in India and abroad. After only one and a half years into the development of the Ashram, Captain Sevier passed away, and this brave, greathearted woman remained another 16 years (to about age 70) dedicated to the work of her guru. As the author writes, *"She was a lone British woman, recently widowed, living in an isolated jungle region of British India at the turn of the 20th century, surrounded by a group of monks, practicing Advaita Vedanta."*

Swami Premananda wrote of Mother Sevier, *"Our 'mother' – I mean Mrs. Sevier – is an example of superb renunciation. Her husband, too, was of the same type...What an exquisite ideal of self-sacrifice they showed!"*

Being so remote, the ashram, under her motherly care, became a refuge for the poor villagers of the vicinity in need of medicine, advice, and other help. Almost immediately a charitable dispensary was set up that developed over the years into the Advaita Ashram Charitable Hospital of today. She was known as "mother" to the inmates of the ashram and those she served. The villagers called her "Bhagavati," a name for the Divine Mother. About her Swami Vivekananda wrote circa 1899, *"And Mrs. Sevier, because she did not care for honors, has the worship of thousands today; and when she is dead millions will remember her as one of the great benefactresses of the poor Indians..."* Indeed, she funded the establishment of two ashrams, donated generously to Belur Math and to various swamis for education, special projects, and personal needs. She also gave money to many ashram staff and villagers.

The first half of *Mother of Mayavati* focuses on Charlotte's early life and yearnings, then details the struggles and successes of establishing the Advaita Ashrama. Great care is given to show the development of her practical and spiritual motherhood and how that filtered through all her daily activities as a Trustee and manager of the ashram and its activities. Throughout the biographical portion, we also see the relations between Charlotte and the direct disciples of Sri Ramakrishna, as well as with the Vivekananda's other Western women disciples, such as Sister Nivedita and Sister Christine. They formed a special bond and supported each other in their efforts to spread Vivekananda's teachings and help uplift the poor of India. The second half includes appendices of her articles printed in *Prabuddha Bharata*, an English language journal of the Order.

Mother Sevier's story fills in many details about the young Order, Swami Vivekananda's relationships with his disciples, and the activities of the residents of Advaita Ashrama on behalf of Vedanta and the Indian people. Exceptionally beautiful and historically significant photos of that time are also included.

In The Divine Realm
By Swami Apurvananda
Advaita Ashrama, 2016, 376 pages

In The Divine Realm is the reminiscences of Swami Apurvananda (1900 – 1990), a monk of the Ramakrishna Order who spent his young life in the company of Sri Ramakrishna's direct disciples and the Holy Mother, Sri Sarada Devi. The title of this book aptly describes the incomparable atmosphere surrounding the Ishvarakotis of Sri Ramakrishna and offers readers the opportunity to vicariously imbibe their transformative influence. Originally published in Bengali in 1991, this new English translation is beautifully rendered.

The author first encountered the lives of Sri Ramakrishna, Swami Vivekananda, and Swami Shivananda when he was 16 years old and had just joined an Indian revolutionary party. Hearing about their lives and teachings from an older devotee immediately turned his mind from political goals toward the goal of Realization and selfless service. In a series of auspicious events, he met Mahapurush Maharaj, received initiation from the Holy Mother, and became a monastic member of the Ramakrishna Order. The description of Holy Mother's initiation is enthralling. Swami Apurvananda later became Mahapurush' attendant, and served him throughout his tenure as the second president of the Order until his mahasamadhi. His position as attendant made it possible for him to recount these priceless memories and intimate details of Swami Shivananda.

The author's stories of how Mahapurush guided him and the other young brahmacharis are among the essential take-aways of this book. Living and serving the direct disciples, for whom the Great Master was all in all, who literally experienced his divine presence everywhere and in everything, infused the young men with conviction that every act of service was received directly by Sri Ramakrishna himself.

"Joyfully serve the Master. Know the other monastic members to be your brothers and near and dear ones. Serve the Master and do your spiritual practices with all sincerity. Nothing belongs to you; everything is God's. The Math and all the works associated with it are God's; we are only His servants – this should be clearly understood. The more your mind is immersed in thoughts of God, the better you will realize this." "...The Lord Himself arranges for His service; we only experience His glory and are blessed."

"Look here, my son, if the Master is true, we too are true. Whatever I say is nothing but the truth; we have not come to cheat people. If we sink, you will sink with us; but by His grace we have realized that we shall never sink, nor will you."

There are countless stories, previously untold, concerning the doings and teachings of Swamis Shivananda, Brahmananda, Saradananda, Turiyananda, Shubodhananda, Abedhananda, Premananda and others. This book is a precious record of the early days of the Ramakrishna Order and the challenging yet swift and natural development of its mission of Self-Realization and service of God in human beings. It brings us so close to these great souls that we can feel their pure and powerful influence that caused beings to shift from worldliness to spiritual striving, and from spiritual striving to actual attainment.

Annapurna Sarada

Sri Sarada Devi and Her Divine Play
by Swami Chetanananda
Vedanta Society of St Louis, 2015
Paperback, 876 pgs, illustrated

Sri Sarada Devi and Her Divine Play immerses the reader in *Liladhyan*, meditation on the Divine Sport of an incarnation of God. This practice unerringly strengthens devotion and faith by awakening the divine Presence within one's heart.

In his fine preface, Swami Chetanananda writes: "After translating Swami Saradananda's *Sri Ramakrishna Lilaprasangha* (*Sri Ramakrishna and His Divine Play*), I felt my work was half done. Just as a theatre audience becomes irritated and begins shouting if an interesting drama ends midway, so I thought the devoted followers of Ramakrishna and Holy Mother might be annoyed with me if I did not complete the whole drama."

Personally, I had not realized how much I had been yearning for a book such as this on the Holy Mother, Sri Sarada Devi, nor had I considered that one was even possible. The author has compiled an excellent selection of excerpts from previous biographies and reminiscences, exquisitely cast in a fresh setting to highlight important themes. Then, he has filled out the Mother's life with an abundance of enthralling new stories and teachings translated from Bengali, relying primarily on eye-witness accounts. In this book of 876 absorbing pages, Swami Chetanananda skillfully performs the duty of a *sutradhara*, one who keeps the thread of the story clearly presented, by writing introductions, commentaries, and elucidations so the reader will extract the most from Sri Sarada Devi's life. Frankly speaking, a book like this is not to be reviewed, but revered.

For those who are not acquainted with Sri Sarada Devi, she was the spiritual consort of Sri Ramakrishna Paramahamsa, and after his passing in 1886 became the spiritual head of the lineage and Order he brought together, which today has centers all over the world. Yet, it was not merely her status as his wife that made her thus, but increasing recognition by Sri Ramakrishna's disciples and others that she embodied the singular Reality known as the Divine Mother of the Universe. Though a simple village woman, nearly illiterate, a purdah widow observing caste rules, she nonetheless had the ability to penetrate to the heart of any issue, set aside socio-cultural strictures instantly as the circumstances required, and bestow spiritual insight with a look, a touch, a thought. She embodies the compassionate Motherhood of God.

Those who are acquainted or even well-acquainted with Holy Mother's life will revel in all the new details. It is an utter banquet that can satisfy our hunger and thirst for her divine presence and love. She simultaneously connects intimately to our daily lives through her ordinary activities and experiences, while engulfing us with the magnificence of her imminent divine reality. Did we long to hear more about her life with Sri Ramakrishna? It is given! Did we secretly wonder how she could be so attached to domestic family issues and still be looked upon as the final word in spirituality by Swamis Vivekananda, Brahmananda, and others? It is there in absolutely edifying examples. Perhaps we wanted to know about her samadhis, her wisdom words, or more about her relationships with Western women devotees – it is provided! And along with so much more, as well.

For Western women treading the path of spirituality, Holy Mother's life is a honeycomb of inspiration and loving wisdom. She immediately transcends the veil of culture and embraces us as her own; and in her vast spiritual affection, we understand the value of simplicity, what dedication, freedom, and spirituality really are, and how to be true every moment of our lives. Margaret Noble, known as Sister Nivedita, spent many intimate hours with Holy Mother and wrote on two different occasions: *"She really is, under the simplest, most unassuming guise, one of the strongest and greatest of women."* And also,*"…the stateliness of her courtesy and her great open mind are almost as wonderful as her sainthood. I have never known her to hesitate in giving utterance to large and generous judgement, however new or complex might be the question put before her."*

In the earlier works of Holy Mother's life, we have been introduced to her modesty and bashfulness and become acquainted with a selection of her simple and penetrating teachings. Written and/or edited as these are by the monks of the Ramakrishna Order, one cannot fail to notice and respond inwardly to the profound reverence for her as the *"Sangha Janani"* (Mother of the Sangha) and the *Shakti* (Power) of Sri Ramakrishna. But one also might have felt a certain reticence to exposing her fully to the public. She kept herself veiled, after all, even before her spiritual sons. Now, after nearly 100 years since Holy Mother left her physical form, it seems she has compassionately decided to put aside this veil so we may gaze with love and fascinated awe upon her entire life in intimate and astounding detail — and the result is this book. As Swami Chetanananda writes, "I deeply felt that this project would help me accomplish two goals: first, it would engage my mind in meditating on Holy Mother for a long period; second, her sublime life and practical teachings would inspire people in this joyless world."

"Let me tell you something. No one will understand me as long as I am alive. They will know only afterwards." - Sri Sarada Devi

Our gratitude will ever be to the author for bringing us into his liladhyan upon Sri Sarada Devi, the Holy Mother.

Annapurna Sarada

SRV Associations — Babaji's Teaching Schedule, 2017

| **SRV Hawai'i Administrative Office**
PO Box 1364
Honoka'a, HI 96727 | **SRV Associations'**
website: www.srv.org
email: srvinfo@srv.org
Phone: 808-990-3354 | **SRV Oregon**
1922 SE 42nd Ave.,
Portland, OR 97215
Ph: 503-774-2410 | **SRV San Francisco**
465 Brussels Street
San Francisco, CA 94134
Ph: 415-468-4680 |

February/March, 2017

SRV San Francisco (Meditation, 6 to 7 am)
- 2/24 Fri 7:00pm Arati/Satsang with Babaji
- 2/25 Sat 9:30am Class: Amrita Bindu Upanisad
- 7:00pm Sri Ramakrishna Birth Puja/Sivaratri
- 2/26 Sun 9:30am Class: Amrita Bindu Upanisad

SRV Oregon (Call for meditation times)
- 3/3 Fri 7:00pm Satsang with Babaji
- 3/4 Sat 9:30am Class: Adhyatma Upanisad
- 6:00pm Sri Ramakrishna Birth Puja
- 3/5 Sun 9:30am Class: Adhyatma Upanisad
- 3/8 Wed 7:00pm Principles of the Upanisads, with Anurag
- 3/9 - 3/13 — SRV Winter Retreat, Seattle, WA

SRV Winter Retreat, 3/9 - 3/13, Seattle, WA
Subject: Advaita Vedanta in a Jivanmukta
(arrive Thursday night 9th, depart Monday 13th at noon)
For details, see Retreat Pages

May, 2017

SRV San Francisco (Meditation, 6 to 7 am)
- 5/12 Fri 7:00pm Arati/Satsang
- 5/13 Sat 9:30am Class: Amrita Bindu Upanisad
- 7:00pm SRV Puja
- 5/14 Sun 9:30am Class: Amrita Bindu Upanisad

SRV Oregon (Call for meditation times)
- 5/17 Wed 7:00pm Principles of the Upanisads, with Anurag
- 5/19 Fri 7:00pm Satsang with Babaji
- 5/20 Sat 9:30am Class: Adhyatma Upanisad
- 6:00pm Shodashi Puja
- 5/21 Sun 9:30am Class: Adhyatma Upanisad
- 5/24 Wed 7:00pm Principles of the Upanisads, with Anurag
- 5/25 - 5/29 Memorial Day Retreat

Memorial Day Weekend Retreat — 5/25 - 29
Subject: Province of the Enlightened:
Glimpses & Gleanings of Gaudapada
Location: Windwood Waters (Wind River Region)
(arrive Thursday evening 25th, depart Monday 29th at noon)
For details, see Retreat Pages

Visit srv.org for all retreat details
Weekend Classes webcasted, 9:30 am to 12:30 pm, Pacific Time

July, 2017

SRV San Francisco (Meditation, 6 to 7 am)
- 7/6 Fri SRV SF Summer Retreat Begins at Foresthill, CA.

SRV American River Retreat over Gurupurnima
July 6th, eve - July 12th, noon – Foresthill, CA
Subject: Sri Ramakrishna's Radiant Road to Reality
Plus: Chanting, Memorization, & Discourse on select Stotrams
Plus: Planned Film on Swami Vivekananda
(arrive Thursday night 6th, depart Wednesday 12th at noon)
For details, see Retreat Pages

SRV Oregon (Call for meditation times)
- 7/15 Sat 9:30am Class: Adhyatma Upanisad
- 6:00pm SRV Puja, Siva Puja
- 7/16 Sun 9:30am Class: Adhyatma Upanisad
- 7/19 Wed 7:00pm Principles of the Upanisads, with Anurag
- 7/21 Fri 6:00pm Open Seminar Satsang with Babaji
- 7/21 - 23 Weekend Seminar

SRV Weekend Seminar with Satsang, 7/21 - 7/23
Subject: Meditation: Its Purpose & Practice
Friday Satsang at 7 pm, & 2 classes Sat., 2 classes Sun.

- 7/26 Wed 7:00pm Principles of the Upanisads, with Anurag
- 7/29 Sat 9:30am Class: Adhyatma Upanisad
- 6:00pm SRV Puja, Siva Puja
- 7/30 Sun 9:30am Class: Adhyatma Upanisad

September/October, 2017

SRV San Francisco (Meditation, 6 to 7 am)
- 9/22 Fri 7:00pm Arati/Satsang
- 9/23 Sat 9:30am Class: Amrita Bindu Upanisad
- 7:00pm Durga Puja
- 9/24 Sun 9:30am Class: Amrita Bindu Upanisad

SRV Oregon (Call for meditation times)
- 9/29 Fri 7:00pm Satsang with Babaji
- 9/30 Sat 9:30am Class: Adhyatma Upanisad
- 6:00pm Durga Puja
- 10/1 Sun 9:30am Class: Adhyatma Upanisad
- 10/4 Wed 7:00pm Principles of the Upanisads, with Anurag
- 10/5 - 10/9 "Discoverer's" Day Retreat

SRV Fall Retreat — 10/5 - 10/9
Over Columbus Day Weekend, Seattle, WA
SRV Durga-Lakshmi-Kali Retreat
Subject: The Seven Goddess Upanisads
(arrive Thursday evening 5th, depart Monday 9th at noon)
For details, see Retreat Pages

* **Vedanta for Teens & Children**
at SRV Oregon and SRV San Francisco
Contact Annapurna Sarada — Ph: 808-990-3354

SRV Associations — Babaji's Teaching Schedule, 2017
SRV Hawai'i Ashram, Big Island

Annual Hawaii Retreat
Title: Precipitous Ascent into Higher Awareness
Location: Puna, Big Island of Hawaii
April 21-24, 2017

Sunday Live Streaming Classes, 2:30 - 5:30pm
Hawai'i SRV Ashram   Directions: Call: 808-990-3354

- **The Eternal Companion**
  January 29, & Feb 5, 12th
- **Swami Aseshananda: My Guru's Teachings**
  March 26, & April 2, 9, 16, 23, 30th
- **The Importance of Yoga's Seventh Limb**
  June 11, 18, 25th
- **Negligence of Brahman & Doorways to Yoga**
  August 13, 20, 27, & September 3, 10th
- **Sadhana: Destroying the Rust of Spiritual Life**
  October 22, 29, & November 5, 12, 19, 26th

Notice:
Our 2017 schedule is subject to change.
Please check the calendar on our website
www.srv.org
and sign our e-list at classes for notifications
or read our e-newsletter, Mundamala.
You can also contact your local SRV center:
Hawaii & Oregon: 808-990-3354
San Francisco: 415-468-4680

Check www.srv.org for Hawaii retreats
or see our Retreats Pages in the back of this issue

Sign up for:
- SRV Magazine: Nectar of Non-Dual Truth
- Raja Yoga email study with Babaji
- SRV's Facebook page
- SRV's YouTube channel: Teaching videos

* Please call or inquire about our Children's Classes
Contact Annapurna Sarada — Phone 808-990-3354

SRV Hawai'i Administrative Office:
PO Box 1364
Honoka'a, HI 96727
Ph: 808-990-3354

SRV Associations' website:
www.srv.org
email:
srvinfo@srv.org

See our SRV Facebook Page   facebook.com/srv.vedanta

SRV Associations Website
www.srv.org
srvinfo@srv.org

SRV On The Web
Visit www.srv.org to find:

SRV's Livestream Channel
Webcast Time Zone Schedule
SRV's YouTube Channel Class Series
- Advaita of the Avatars
- Devotion of Nonseparation
- The Wisdom Particle
- Non-Touch Yoga
- Shakta-Advaita-vada
- Satsangs with Babaji

Explore our Website links to find:
- Sanskrit Chants to learn/practice
- Devotional Songs
- Audio Discourses

Teachings:
- Articles
- Raja Yoga Sutras Study
- SRV's Teachings for Youth/Children
- Podcasts

Magazine:
- Order back issues of Nectar
- View our online archive of Nectar
- Order back issues of Nectar

News & Events
- Mundamala – SRV's e-newsletter
  Full of teachings and more

SRV Associations — Retreats for 2017

SRV Winter/Spring Retreat
March 9th - 13th, 2017, Seattle, Washington
Retreat Topic: Advaita Vedanta in a Jivanmukta

The most overlooked and under-appreciated being on earth today is the rare living liberated soul, long heralded in India as the only one really able guide both the masses, and particularly, that equally rare sincere seeker after Truth who seizes the holy feet of that personage and never lets go until Enlightenment dawns on the mind. This unique retreat is a chance for such sincere souls to gather to hear and contemplate the winsome words of illumination spoken by Swami Aseshanandaji Maharaj for over forty years in the West up until his passing into samadhi in the 1990's. This unique being had a message for America that was not only geared towards raising the spiritual consciousness of its people, but that was keenly in touch and in tune with the internal causes that have placed this country both at the head of the world's power and privilege, and which are at the source of much of its confusion and suffering as well.

"The book of life here on earth always reads the same, and is telling. For the worldly man it reads, 'Today on the throne of France, tomorrow food for worms.' But for the spiritual person it reads, 'Today a carpenter's son, tomorrow worshipped by millions of people.'"

"Western man accepts objective experience only. However, if you look, in meditation, behind the phenomenal universe, you will see the Infinite Spirit, the Eternal Subject, the Divine Mother."
  – Swami Aseshanandaji Maharaj

Texts/other: *Ten new charts on the select teachings of Swami Aseshanandaji* **Location:** Seattle, Washington
Arrival: Thursday, March 9th, after dinner and by 9:00pm **Departure:** Monday, March 13th, at 12:00 noon
Tuition (all inclusive): $350; students $175 **Registration:** Starts now. Tuition is due by <u>March 1st</u>
Financial hardship? Call 808-990-3354 **Register by email:** srvinfo@srv.org or by phone 808-990-3354

SRV Spring Retreat Over Memorial Day Weekend
May 25th – 29th, 2017, Wind River region, Stevenson, Washington
Subject: Province of the Enlightened; Glimpses of Gaudapada

The enlightened luminary and nondual philosopher, Lord Gaudapada, holds much more than just his fame as the author of the lucid nondual commentary (karika) on the Mandukya Upanisad, he also was the paramaguru of Shankara, and the spiritual preceptor of Patanjali in his lifetime as Govindapada. *Glimpses of Gaudapada* will take us there, into the great mind of this spiritual phenomenon, who somehow makes the otherwise abstract Advaita Vedanta the most natural state of mind available to mankind.

In SRV's Spring retreat at Windwood Waters near the Columbia River Gorge in Washington state, the underground river of Advaita Vedanta will surface once again, bringing its healing Waters of Life upwards in a fountain of Truth to nourish all thirsty souls, just as it did in Gaudapada's time in India in 500 A.D.

Location: Windwood Waters retreat site near Stevenson, WA
Arrival: Thursday, May 25th, between 4:00 & 9:00 pm
Departure: Monday, May 29th, 12:00 noon
Registration: Starts now. Tuition and lodging fees are due by May 7th
Register by email: srvinfo@srv.org or by phone 808-990-3354
Costs: Tuition and meals: $390; Students:: $200 (lodging additional)
Lodging: private room single, $240; private room shared with 1 - 2 others, $160/person;
Semi-private lodge sleeping, $120*; Tenting, $80* *bring your own bedding/towels

SRV American River Retreat, 2016
July 6th – 12th, 2017, Forest Hill, CA
- Sri Ramakrishna's Radiant Road to Reality
Plus: Planned Movie of Swami Vivekananda

- Live in holy company for a full week – meditating, studying, serving, and growing together.
- Each morning begins with chanting from the Bhagavad Gita prior to meditation.
- Daily classes include essential teachings of Yoga, Vedanta, Tantra, and Sankhya.
- Afternoons include explorations and swimming/sunning along the American River.
- Afternoon Chela Dharma class for teens and young adults.
- Evening devotions at the altar, singing and chanting, meditation, and satsang.
- Spiritual Music Features: Chanting and memorization of Sri Ramakrishna Mangalam, Sri Ramakrishna Suprabhatam, & the Ramakrishna Chalisa.

Location: Private land in Foresthill, California near the American River
Arrival: Arrive by 6pm, Thursday evening, July 6th
Last day of retreat: Wednesday, July 12 (approximately noon, clean up follows)
Tuition: all inclusive
   Adults: $636 (full retreat) $275 (weekend, arrive Friday) $110/day
   Children/Students: $300 (full retreat) $140 (weekend, arrive Friday) $55/day
Registration: starts now and tuition is due by Friday, June 30th
Financial hardship? Call 808-990-3354 to discuss options
Register by email: srvinfo@srv.org or by phone 808-990-3354

Autumn Retreat on Discoverer's Day Weekend, Over Lakshmi Puja
October 5th – 9th, 2017, Location: Seattle, Washington
Subject: The Seven Goddess Upanisads: Part 3

Similar to SRV's Fall retreats of 2015/16, wherein the Devi and Sita Upanisads were presented and studied in depth, Babaji will take up another of the Seven Goddess Upanisads for examination and contemplation.

Location: Seattle, Washington
Arrival: Thursday, October 5th after dinner, at 9:00pm
Departure: Monday, October 9th, 12:00 noon
Tuition (all-inclusive): Adults: $350: Students: $175
Registration: Tuition and other fees are due by September 21st

---

Plus: SRV Summer Seminar in 2017
Meditation: Its Purpose & Practice

"As the timepiece on the wall goes on ticking, so too must you continue to meditate. Practice japa and meditate at regular times giving up idleness. And don't just seek God; see God. You can see Him if you strive to attain a pure mind." Sri Sarada Devi

July 21-23 at the SRV Oregon Ashram in Portland
Schedule: July 21: 7:00 PM – Satsang
Saturday, July 22nd: 6:00am – 5:00pm (meditation, breakfast, morning and afternoon classes, dinner)
Sunday, July 23rd: 6:00am – 5:00pm (meditation, breakfast and 1 morning class)
Tuition: $220; student, $110
Accommodations: This is a non-residential seminar
Contact us if you would like assistance with lodging. 808-990-3354 // srvinfo@srv.org
Registration: Tuition due by Sunday, July 16th

The "In The Spirit" Interviews of Lex Hixon

Lex Hixon

From the early 1970's on through the late 1980's, Lex Hixon hosted a radio program in New York City that was unprecedented in its depth, scope, insight and unique creativity. First entitled "In The Spirit," it also later appeared under the titles of "Body/Mind/Spirit," and "Spirit/Mind/Body."

On this long running inspirational program that spanned over two decades and which was duly sponsored in listener-supported fashion on WBAI Radio, Lex interviewed educators, healers, clergy, authors, artists, psychics, spiritual leaders and others.

As a list, the fruit of this selfless work reads like a comprehensive Who's Who of the spiritual, artistic and intellectual heart and mind of both Eastern and Western cultures. With subtle tenderness and insight, though never lacking the penetrating edge which makes for excellent broadcasting, Lex welcomed the orthodox and the unorthodox, the conservative and the radical, the famous and the obscure, the popular and the controversial, the powerful and the humble, the aggressive and the retiring.

Included in this copious series are interviews with gurus, yogis, swamis, priests, roshis, rabbis/rebbes, sheikhs, lamas, rinpoches, poets, musicians, psychics, occultists, authors, writers, teachers, politicians, businessmen and more.

- Over 325 Titles to choose from
- Individual CD's are available
- Trio sets
- Full set prices
- List of all titles available upon request
- Highest quality materials used

"IN THE SPIRIT" CD Trio Sets
Choice selections from the cassette series on CD

Buddhist
B1 - Tibetan
Dalai Lama
Kalu Rinpoche
Trungpa Rinpoche

B2 - Zen
Eido Roshi
Soen Roshi
Maesumi Roshi

B3 - American
Phillip Kapleau
Bernie Glassman
Robert Thurman

Christianity
C1 - Mother Teresa
Padre Pio
Meister Ekhart

Islam/Sufism
IS1 - Sheikh Muzaffer
Guru Bawa
Sheikh Nur Al Jerrahi

Judaism
J1 - Rabbi Shlomo Carlebach
Rebbe Gedalia
Rabbi Zalman Schachter

J2 - Rebbi Meyer Fund
Rabbi Dovid Din
Rabbi Lynn Gotleib

Lex Hixon
H1 - On the Haj
On the Karmapa
On Himself

Professors & Authors
PA1 - Huston Smith
Christopher Isherwood
Jack Cornfield

PA2 - David Spangler
Alan Watts
Alan Ginsberg

Shamanism/Amer. Indian
SI1 - Oh Shinnah
Dhani Thorna
Don Juan

Vedic
V1 - Sri Ramakrishna

V2 - Ramakrishna Order Swamis
Vivekananda
Nikhilananda
Prabhavananda

V3 - Swamis
Dayananda
Muktananda
Satchitananda

V4 - Special Luminaries
Ramana Maharshi
Sri Aurobindo
Krishnamurti

V5 - Spiritual Teachers
Meher Baba
Sri Chinmoy
Ram Das

V6 - Divine Mother of the Universe

Postal Orders: Jai Ma Music, PO Box 380, Paauilo, HI 96776
Email Orders: srvinfo@srv.org
Phone Orders: 808-990-3354
Website: www.srv.org

Advaita-satya-amritam

NECTAR
Of Non-Dual Truth

Donation/Order Form
Suggested donation $15 per issue

Nectar #33 is available for free if you write, email, or call for a copy by January 15, 2018.
Your generous donations make Nectar available to others.
Those who donate $15 or more for the next issue will be added our subscribers list.

☐ Please send me/my friend a free copy of the next issue of Nectar.
☐ Send me ____ copies to give to friends, Spiritual Centers, or a business of my choice. (fill out back of form)
☐ I want to make sure there are future issues of Nectar ($200 and up)

Nectar needs sustaining donors! ($500 and up) Your gift is tax-deductible.

Please fill out the back side of this form and mail it with your check to:
SRV Associations, PO Box 1364, Honokaa, HI 96727
MasterCard or Visa accepted • Make checks payable to: SRV Associations
808-990-3354 • srvinfo@srv.org • www.srv.org

#32

Advaita-satya-amritam

NECTAR
Of Non-Dual Truth

Donation/Order Form
Suggested donation $15 per issue

Nectar #33 is available for free if you write, email, or call for a copy by January 15, 2018.
Your generous donations make Nectar available to others.
Those who donate $15 or more for the next issue will be added our subscribers list.

☐ Please send me/my friend a free copy of the next issue of Nectar.
☐ Send me ____ copies to give to friends, Spiritual Centers, or a business of my choice. (fill out back of form)
☐ I want to make sure there are future issues of Nectar ($200 and up)

Nectar needs sustaining donors! ($500 and up) Your gift is tax-deductible.

Please fill out the back side of this form and mail it with your check to:
SRV Associations, PO Box 1364, Honokaa, HI 96727
MasterCard or Visa accepted • Make checks payable to: SRV Associations
808-990-3354 • srvinfo@srv.org • www.srv.org

#32

Advaita-satya-amritam

NECTAR
Of Non-Dual Truth

Donation/Order Form
Suggested donation $15 per issue

Nectar #33 is available for free if you write, email, or call for a copy by January 15, 2018.
Your generous donations make Nectar available to others.
Those who donate $15 or more for the next issue will be added our subscribers list.

☐ Please send me/my friend a free copy of the next issue of Nectar.
☐ Send me ____ copies to give to friends, Spiritual Centers, or a business of my choice. (fill out back of form)
☐ I want to make sure there are future issues of Nectar ($200 and up)

Nectar needs sustaining donors! ($500 and up) Your gift is tax-deductible.

Please fill out the back side of this form and mail it with your check to:
SRV Associations, PO Box 1364, Honokaa, HI 96727
MasterCard or Visa accepted • Make checks payable to: SRV Associations
808-990-3354 • srvinfo@srv.org • www.srv.org

#32

Your Information:

Name: _____
Address: _____
City, State, Zip: _____
Email: _____

Additional Address: (please use a sheet of paper for more addresses)

Name: _____
Address: _____
City, State, Zip: _____
Email: _____

Do you wish to pay by Mastercard or Visa?
Card No.: _____ **Amount:** _____
Exp. date: _____ **Phone no.:** _____
Signature: _____

Questions? call SRV Associations: 808-990-3354

Your Information:

Name: _____
Address: _____
City, State, Zip: _____
Email: _____

Additional Address: (please use a sheet of paper for more addresses)

Name: _____
Address: _____
City, State, Zip: _____
Email: _____

Do you wish to pay by Mastercard or Visa?
Card No.: _____ **Amount:** _____
Exp. date: _____ **Phone no.:** _____
Signature: _____

Questions? call SRV Associations: 808-990-3354

Your Information:

Name: _____
Address: _____
City, State, Zip: _____
Email: _____

Additional Address: (please use a sheet of paper for more addresses)

Name: _____
Address: _____
City, State, Zip: _____
Email: _____

Do you wish to pay by Mastercard or Visa?
Card No.: _____ **Amount:** _____
Exp. date: _____ **Phone no.:** _____
Signature: _____

Questions? call SRV Associations: 808-990-3354

www.ingramcontent.com/pod-product-compliance
Lightning Source LLC
Chambersburg PA
CBHW080024110526
44587CB00021BA/3837